ESCAPING
ILLUSIONS

THERESE HECKENKAMP

Ivory Tower Press

www.ivorytowerpress.com

Cover design by 100 Covers

Published by
Ivory Tower Press
www.ivorytowerpress.com

BOOKS BY THERESE HECKENKAMP

Frozen Footprints Series

Frozen Footprints
After the Thaw
Escaping Illusions

Standalone Novels

Past Suspicion
The Butterfly Recluse
Sleep Deprived

For my brother, Jerome.
Thanks for a magical childhood.

Illusion

It was there and then it wasn't—
Like the memory of a dream—
When everything you see
Isn't what it seems.
But somehow I caught a glimpse
In the half instant it was there,
While the rest of the world
Politely disappeared.

It was like some sort of promise—
A wisp of gossamer—
Had floated out to meet me
Upon a gauzy blur.
It shimmered so enticingly
Like a spiderweb so fine,
And it danced before my eyes
In a delicate design.

It was rivaling reality—
Shifting like the sand—
And it tantalized my mind
Till it was more than I could stand.
I had to touch this thing,
To prove that it was there,
So I reached out my hand—
But all I touched was air.

One

It had to be tonight. I'd waited far too many years already.

My mind processed my impulsive plan, paying little attention to the bedtime story I was reading my daughter.

"No, that's not what it says, Mommy. You skipped the best part."

Ella, my ever-observant six-year-old, pointed to the page and recited the words so sweetly it made my heart ache. "'And the princess married the prince and they lived happily ever after.'"

The statement soured my stomach, but Ella sighed contentedly beside me on the bed.

"How'd I miss that?" I whispered past a catch in my throat. "Silly me."

Lying, misleading book.

She didn't marry the prince, I wanted to say. *He was not really the nice man he pretended to be. The princess was smart. She took care of herself and lived safely ever after.*

What more could anyone want?

It sure beat waiting around to be rescued from a fire-breathing dragon. What nonsense.

But Ella loved it. She was innocent, trusting.

I'd do anything to preserve that.

I closed the book, set it on her nightstand, and dimmed her rose lamp to a gentle glow. Still not dim enough to blot out the ugly hole in her pink wall.

"Mommy?" Ella said. "Don't forget prayers."

I patted her hand. "We won't." We'd need them more than ever tonight.

"Angel of God, my guardian dear . . ." Ella started with her favorite prayer, then went on to ask Jesus for sweet dreams and snow.

"And make Daddy nice," she added, almost as an afterthought. She plucked my sleeve. Insecurities flickered like dark moths behind her big eyes. "Sleep with me tonight?"

"Of course." I snuggled down beside her. She didn't have to know I wouldn't be closing my eyes.

She touched my cheek, fingers feather soft, hesitant on my fresh bruise. "Does it hurt?"

"No." Not much. I'd had worse.

Why'd you make me do that, Brook? Why?

Blocking the memory of his voice, I stroked Ella's blond hair back from her face and squeezed her shoulder gently. "How about you?"

"A little." She curled against me. "Daddy said he was sorry."

He always did.

"He said he didn't mean to hurt us."

I heard the question in her voice. Her need for me to

confirm we'd never encounter that scary version of him again.

I understood her need to believe it.

I used to believe it, made all the excuses.

It was harder to hide his blowups now that she was older. But her getting caught in the violence—this was a first.

It had to be the last. My hands fisted. I was done making excuses.

At twenty-nine, I couldn't keep myself safe. Why had I believed I could protect her?

Whether he'd meant to hurt us or not, he had. That's what counted.

"Don't worry, honey. He won't ever do that again." I'd make certain.

Satisfied, her eyes drooped and she sucked her thumb, a habit I thought she'd broken. Her breathing turned steady, soothing. I waited.

Listened.

Waited some more.

But Connor's footsteps never creaked up the stairs. I could just make out the low hum of the TV downstairs. Good. He'd likely fall asleep on the couch, pretzel crumbs on his lap and a beer can on the side table.

At midnight, I eased off the mattress and unzipped Ella's ladybug backpack, then slid in clothes, underwear, a hairbrush, and her favorite stuffed animal.

I crept to the master bedroom and tugged my own

backpack from behind out-of-season clothing—the bag I'd used for one semester of college before I'd dropped out and shackled myself to Connor.

I added essentials and the envelope of cash I'd slowly accumulated over the last four years. I'd tucked away the first bill after that first hit, hoping I would someday have the guts—the sense—to do this.

How shameful that it had taken Ella getting hurt to spur me to action.

Leaving the backpack in the closet, I crept down to the kitchen. Numbers glowed on the microwave clock. Silver handles protruded from the chunky knife block on the counter. From here I could see Connor's dark shape sprawled on the couch, TV lights flickering over him, confirming his eyes were closed. Still, I took a glass from the cupboard and filled it with water. Took a sip.

"Connor?" I moved closer. Had to be sure. "Are you awake?"

Too bad he wasn't the kind of man who snored.

"Connor?"

The lack of response would have to be enough.

Time to go.

Two

Ella kicked the back of my seat, jolting me. "Where are we going, Mommy?"

Good question.

I stared at the asphalt, the seemingly endless Wisconsin highway illuminated only by headlights as we rumbled on, leaving our hometown of Bloomington far behind.

This trip had never been about the destination. Once my foot had pressed the pedal, it didn't want to let up. There was something incredibly encouraging about putting distance between us and Connor. Each new mile made it less likely he'd find us.

Reason enough to keep driving.

My tension remained high, my heart racing. The reality that I was finally leaving was tainted by fear that my escape was an illusion—that somehow he'd find me, stop me.

"Mommy," Ella repeated, "where are we going?"

"On a little trip, sweetie." I put on a bright face, as if she could see me. Reflex. "Doesn't that sound fun?"

"A water park?" Her voice was hopeful, yet suspicious.

"Are we going to a water park?"

What a thing to long for on a freezing January night. I cracked a smile.

"Or Disney World?" Another kick hit my seat.

"Not quite that fun, not yet." Maybe someday. I glanced in the rearview mirror. Headlights glared back at me. The same ones I'd seen for miles? The vehicle kept getting closer. I frowned and switched lanes.

A minute later, the vehicle did the same.

Anxiety filled me. I pressed the gas and surged forward. At the last possible second, I pulled onto an exit.

The vehicle swerved as if about to follow, despite the barrier, then straightened and whizzed past.

My jaw clenched. Sweat chilled me. Overreaction? Perhaps. I'd been well conditioned.

The erratic driving might have nothing to do with me and everything to do with the late hour and bar closing time.

But I shouldn't assume anything.

I took some random turns. No need to worry about getting lost when I had no firm destination in mind. I wouldn't head anywhere logical, anywhere I'd ever been before. Certainly not back to Creekside, where Connor and I'd met, even though I had friends there. I wouldn't rope them into my drama. That would be the first place Connor would look.

Not to Aunt Bea's home, either, where I'd spent a short, happy year before she passed.

And certainly not to my parents' place, if they even still lived there. They'd disowned me when I'd become pregnant with Ella. They would say my misfortune served me right. And that was if they'd even talk to me.

Ella groaned. "I'm sick of being in the car."

"Try to go back to sleep."

"I can't," she whined. Tiredness always made her shrill. "I'm hungry. And I need to go potty."

I glanced at the time. I'd really hoped to drive straight through the night.

"Mom*meee*. I have to go *now*."

No sign of a gas station, but I did spot a motel. Which left me about five seconds to make my decision.

I turned in. We could both use some sleep. My brain had been firing fight-or-flight reactions too long. My body craved rest.

Ella sniffed. "This doesn't look like a fun place."

I pictured her peering disapprovingly at the weathered building, the scraggly trees, the too-bright sign, which appeared a little too proud of its vacancy status.

"It's just a place to sleep. Doesn't a cozy bed sound nice?"

I circled the lot and parked where our car couldn't be spotted from the road, then scanned the area and waited a minute before unlocking and opening my door, then Ella's. I slung each of our backpacks over my shoulders.

Ella reached for me, and I scooped her up and carried her on my hip like a toddler. I welcomed her weight. My only baby. No longer a baby at all. That fact still sometimes shocked me, as did my irrational sense of loss. In different circumstances, I would've loved to have given her a sibling.

She nestled her head against me and I tightened my grip.

"Will you sleep in my bed?" she asked. "All night?"

"You bet," I said into her ear, making her giggle. I loved how her messy hair tickled me like an unruly feather duster.

I paid in cash, grabbed a few bags of cheese crackers from the dented vending machine in the lobby, then opened our door with the key card. I quickly shut it behind us and set the chain. Hauled in a deep breath.

We soon sat cross-legged on the bed, Ella nibbling crackers, scattering crumbs. She squinted around the room.

"Isn't this fun?" I asked. "It's like a midnight picnic." Never mind that it was closer to two a.m.

"It would be more fun with ice cream." She shot me a hopeful look.

I suppressed a smirk. "Maybe tomorrow."

"Promise?"

I hesitated. Could I? I never made promises anymore. Too hard to know if I could keep them. I was never the one in control of anything. But this time, I would make it happen. No matter what tomorrow brought, it would finally contain freedom.

"I promise."

After brushing off the comforter, I pulled the bedding back and climbed in beside Ella. She frowned at the door and spoke in a cautious tone. "Is Daddy going to come on our trip?"

I stared at the chain lock. Prayed it was strong. "Do you want him to?"

She poked her thumb to her lips. "If he's fun and nice."

Such a great "if." One no one could guarantee.

Her lashes fluttered downward. She appeared almost asleep when her eyes popped back open.

"Do I have to say bedtime prayers again? I already said them at our house."

I patted her cheek. "You're good. Go to sleep." I'd pray enough for the both of us.

Somewhere between my thanks for our successful getaway and my plea for continued protection, I slipped into drowsiness, my arm still around Ella.

A cautious but wonderful measure of relief washed over me.

Maybe the hardest part of our escape was over.

* * *

"Open up!"

Shouting and pounding pierced my unconsciousness. Ella whimpered and pushed against me as if she would burrow right through me.

Confused, I cracked my gritty eyes. Light seeped from the edges of an unfamiliar curtain-covered window.

"Open up, Brook! I know you're in there." A fist hammered the door.

Connor.

He'd found us.

I flew to my feet, grabbed my phone. Cold air and fear prickled my skin.

"Open the door or I'll break it down." The chain rattled.

My sleep-fogged mind cleared. No, not Connor. The voice was almost his, but not quite. It belonged to his older brother, Ian.

Hardly an improvement.

I marched forward and yelled through the door. "Stop it! You're scaring Ella. I'm not going to open up, so go away."

"We'll get you out of there one way or another, you—" His language made me gasp and rush to cover Ella's ears.

As I held her to my side, she stared wide-eyed at the door, as if worried a monster might pop through.

I had to keep that from happening.

Though I'd only heard Ian, Connor was surely lurking, ready to strike.

How had they found me?

Shaking myself, I projected my voice. "I'm calling the police. I'll tell them everything." The manipulation. The abuse.

"They're already on their way." Ian's voice sounded crazed. "They're not going to protect you." He made a growling noise and attacked the door again. "You're gonna pay for killing Connor."

Three

I pulled away from the door as if it had flown open and smacked me. My hands mashed Ella's ears.

"Ow!" She wiggled from my grasp.

More pounding shook the door. "You hear me?"

My mouth gaped. Strong, fierce Connor. "He's dead?" I rasped the words quietly through the door, trying to spare Ella.

"Yeah, *dead*. That's what happens when you stab someone with a butcher knife, you psycho!"

"Ian, hey . . ." A new voice.

I peered through the peephole, saw Connor's friend Dane race to Ian's side. "Hey, this isn't the way, man. You're only scaring her."

"Like I give a crap." Ian lunged at the door. "When I get my hands on her—"

"You'll never get her to come out like that." Dane gripped Ian's shoulder, his face agitated. He turned to the door as if knowing I was glued to the peephole.

"Brook? It's Dane." His calm voice flipped something inside me. A small comfort amid the disbelief and horror.

Dane. He'd always been kind. A good influence on

Connor, who'd always been nicer to me when he was around.

My fingers pressed against the door. "Is it true? Is Connor really . . . ?"

Dane glanced down and cleared his throat. Seemed to be gathering himself. "Yeah, he's gone."

I stepped back, shook my head. "I didn't do it." Much as I'd grown to resent and fear Connor, I could never—would never—do such a brutal thing. My body trembled.

"Tell us what happened," Ian yelled. "You owe me that."

"I can't tell you, because I don't know. I left with Ella last night. That's all. When he was sleeping." My voice dropped. "He was sleeping."

I turned, struck by Ella's presence. How had I forgotten? She stood frozen, hands twisting her stuffed bunny's ear. How much had she heard? How much did she understand?

"Is Daddy okay?" Her wide eyes pleaded.

God, please. Poor Ella. Swallowing a sob, I swept her into my arms. Poor girl, poor baby.

I'd wanted us free of Connor's clutches, but not like this.

Ella broke into tears, and I struggled to stem my own.

"Brook, you need to tell us more." Dane's voice still sounded patient, but strained. "Why did you leave?"

"I—" The words stuck in my throat.

"The police are here," Ian shouted. "They'll get it out

of you, you lying, murdering—"

My hands flew again to Ella's ears. "Stop! Don't you care about your niece? She can hear you, you heartless brute."

But losing my temper would only feed Ella's fears. She needed comfort, love, not more anger. I lowered my voice, held her to my heart, and whispered, "It'll be okay, sweetie. You'll be okay."

As for me, that was yet to be seen. Sirens shrieked, emphasizing that fact.

I couldn't let them pin this on me and take me away. My daughter needed me.

Car doors slammed. Multiple voices approached. Someone pounded on the door. Not Ian. This banging was different. Controlled, not crazed.

"Police. Open up."

Resolution surged through me. I'd get through this. I had to.

Clutching Ella's hand, fearing they'd tear her from me, I open the door and stood strong, steeling my nerves. "I didn't do it."

A tall female officer met my gaze steadily, but not accusingly. "Brook Morton?"

I nodded.

"We need to ask you some questions."

"Arrest her," Ian hollered, and officers immediately headed for him. Dane tugged him back, shaking his head and saying something.

Ian glared at me and spat on the ground.

"Let's step inside," the officer in front of me said.

"My daughter—"

A younger female officer stepped forward and reached for Ella.

I shielded her with my body. "No, you can't take her."

"Ma'am," said the older officer, who seemed to be in charge. "She'll be fine. She'll be right outside the door with Officer Lindell. Just while we talk."

Her gaze swept me, seemed to say *Work with me*, and I reluctantly nodded.

"No, Mommy! I want to stay with you!" Ella screeched. Tears gushed.

My heart twisted. "Can't I just hold her while we talk?"

The officer pursed her lips, accentuating the accordion-like lines around her mouth. "You don't want her hearing this."

True. I crouched beside Ella, willing calmness into my eyes and words. "Sweetie, I'll be right here, and when I'm done talking, I'll get you. I promise." *God, let it be true.*

The young officer smiled at Ella. "Do you want to see my radio?" She held it up like a tempting toy. "And look inside one of our cool cars?"

I nodded, encouraging Ella. "Go ahead." I kissed her and released her arm. Tried not to regret it.

The older officer stepped closer. "My name's Detective Bale." She gestured to another officer, a slightly overweight man with a small cut on his cheek, like he'd nicked himself shaving. "This is Officer Hurstwood."

They led me inside to the small round table. I focused on a chip in the laminate surface. "Can you tell me what happened? I don't understand—"

Detective Bale pulled out a notebook and pen, then clicked it. "We need to ask you some questions first," she said, though not unkindly.

"Okay." Of course. "Can you just tell me—" I met her clear, steady eyes. "Is—is my husband dead?" The reality—if it was real—still hadn't come close to sinking in.

She paused, then nodded. "Yes. That I can tell you. With certainty."

I closed my eyes.

Oh, Connor.

Emotions flooded me in terrible, forceful waves. Horror gave way to sadness, to confusion . . . to sadness again. After four years of marriage, this was how it ended. For us . . . for him. It wasn't right that I should feel this much relief.

I'd wanted to be free, but not like this . . .

Not by murder.

Four

"I can't believe they didn't arrest her."

The words, spat with contempt by Ian from several yards away, were clearly meant for me. I had no difficulty hearing them above the funeral home's mournful overhead music.

He stood muttering with his mom and dad beside a cluster of flowers, his ears burning an angry red, his tie slightly crooked. Potent lily fragrance filled the room.

I shouldn't have come.

But Ella needed this, didn't she? For closure? I'd grappled with doing what was best, and this was all I knew to offer her for a chance to say goodbye, even if she couldn't truly understand.

I could barely understand, and that was after Detective Bale had filled me in on the events of that terrible morning, how Ian and Dane had encountered the gruesome scene when they arrived to pick Connor up for ice fishing.

A scene so dreadful that I hadn't been able to return to the house for days, not that I wanted to. Crime scene investigators took over. Then the crime scene cleanup.

Though I was spared the awful sight, my imagination made up for it.

What if I hadn't left with Ella that night? Would I, or—heaven forbid—Ella, have been the one to find Connor dead? Worse yet, would we have met the same fate?

Or would it somehow never have happened?

So many questions tormented me.

Ella clung to my leg as I stepped around people, dipping my head to avoid eye contact and, by extension, conversation. The turnout was huge. I couldn't imagine where all these people had come from. Connor had a relatively small circle of friends, mostly from work. And a few, like Dane, from college or high school.

I hated to think it, but most of these people were likely drawn by the sensational way he'd gone. Murder brought out the morbidly fascinated gawkers and gossipers.

It also brought the police. Plainclothes detectives stood by strategically, on the lookout for the killer. The thought chilled me more than comforted me. Would the culprit really show up here? Put on an act and offer false sympathy?

I swallowed. The killer could be anyone.

But that didn't change the fact that most, especially Connor's family, thought it was me. The obvious suspect. Never mind I had a rock-solid alibi from the motel clerk checking me in at the time of the murder. Never mind the authorities had dismissed me as a suspect.

At least, that's what they'd told me. And they wouldn't lie, would they?

Maneuvering past a group of people, I almost toppled one of the many photo memory boards. My hand steadied it just in time, then lingered. There we were, looking like such a happy family. We stood on either side of Ella, age two, pushing her in a swing. Connor always complained about how boring the park was. Yet he wouldn't let me take her there alone.

Our trips lessened, till poor Ella was lucky if we took her more than twice a summer.

Other pictures held similar misleading smiles. In a picture at the zoo, I wore sunglasses although the day was cloudy. Remembering what the glasses hid, my gaze darted to the ornate casket. Closed, of course. The nature of the crime required it.

"I don't like this." Ella wrinkled her nose. "It stinks."

It did. Both literally and figuratively. "I know, honey." I squeezed her hand.

"And there's too many people staring at me."

I felt that too. "We'll sit down soon." Not really a solution, but the best I could offer. Despite the cool, surreptitious stares, I reminded myself not to hang my head. I had nothing to be ashamed of.

My story had checked out. I was in the clear, whether Connor's family believed me or not.

They likely thought I'd staged the scene, which had appeared to be a robbery gone wrong, complete with a broken back window and ransacked rooms. The knife had been wiped clean of any fingerprints. And while Connor's wallet and a few valuables were missing, it was hard to believe that those things had been worth murdering him for.

I didn't think it a stretch to believe he may have made a dangerous enemy, whether through his auto-repair work, time spent in bars, or someplace else. I didn't even know half the places he disappeared to, just knew he was gone at all hours. Vague as that information was, I hoped the police would find it helpful.

I'd also informed them of Connor's violent streak, of our fight, the hole he'd punched in the wall, and they'd seen the bruise on my face—clear motive for my leaving.

Detective Bale told me I should have gone straight to the police. That Connor had an app that tracked my phone. The revelation sent ice through my veins.

Ian had shared the app information with them while he used it to track me down, which was how he and Dane found me so fast.

It shouldn't have surprised me.

Connor had always shared too much with his brother.

I wanted nothing to do with Ian. I'd gladly let him and his parents plan the funeral. I had Ella to focus on, and Connor deserved to have the arrangements made by people who still loved him.

Despite my efforts, my love for him had died years ago. But he was my daughter's father, and for her sake, I tried to grieve his loss.

With heavy steps, I skirted the line of relatives and led Ella to the casket.

"Daddy's in there?" she whispered, concern filling her face. "Isn't it dark?"

I hugged her close. If there were right words for this, I didn't know them. "It's not really him in there—it's just his body." I sucked in a breath and grappled for wisdom. My faith was still so young, barely as old as Ella. "When someone dies, they leave their body. It's like . . . like taking off a snowsuit." Did that make sense? Was it at all comforting, or was it confusing?

She frowned. "So where is he?"

Connor's mother, Barb, swooped in and wrapped an arm around Ella. "In heaven, darling." She eyed me, as if daring me to challenge her.

I closed my eyes and focused on that thought. Connor, in heaven? God was merciful, but also just. While I struggled to understand how the two could mesh, Barb's voice intruded.

"I saw a plate of cookies in the side room, Ella. Would you like to come with me and get some?"

Ella looked at me with a hope I couldn't deny. I nodded. The moment she left my side, I moved away from the casket and followed her with my eyes. Despite the ill will between us, at least Connor's parents adored Ella. She was safe with them.

A group of three young men sidled up to me, and I

recognized them vaguely. The first stood a head taller than the others. "We're real sorry, Brook. He was a fair boss and a good friend."

Work buddies. They'd cleaned up well, with their hair combed and hands scrubbed of usual auto-repair-shop grease.

"Thank you. And thanks for coming."

"Not right, what happened to him." The second man—Sean, I believed—appeared to be battling emotion. The third man, whose name I couldn't recall, avoided my eyes but nodded his condolences. After a few awkward moments, they moved on.

"Brook?"

The new voice, once so familiar, made me turn. Charlene, my old friend and one-time roommate, stood mere steps away, sympathy radiating from her. She hesitated only a second before closing the gap and enveloping me in a hug.

I held on longer than I probably should have, struck by the realization that I hadn't had this kind of connection with another adult in too long.

Charlene had never approved of Connor, knowing he hadn't treated me well. But after he found out Ella was his, he pursued me relentlessly. And I gave in, letting him back in my life, thinking he'd changed, thinking I was giving Ella what was best.

I almost looked past Charlene in hopes of spotting her brother. How ridiculous. Her twin, Max, had better—

more logical—things to do than pop into the service of the man I'd chosen over him.

"I'm so sorry, Brook," Charlene said. "How are you and Gabriella doing?"

If she still knew Ella as Gabriella, it had definitely been too long. "She likes to go by Ella, and we're okay."

Her gaze held, always too perceptive. She'd experienced enough drama in her own life to see through my bluff.

"If there's anything we can do, please let us know." She clasped my hands and lowered her voice. "I mean it. Whether you need help with Ella, food, or somewhere to stay, I'm here for you. Clay too. He sends his condolences. He would've come as well, but the kids are sick."

Kids, plural. The last I'd known, they had one. "Oh, I hope they feel better soon. How many do you have now?"

"Two, a boy and a girl." A smile flickered, her pride and joy obvious in that second. "They keep us busy. But never too busy to help a friend. I know we haven't kept in touch as much as we should have, and I'm sorry."

"Don't be. It's not your fault."

We both knew I was the one who'd let the friendship fade. The fact that I'd once dated Clay used to make me feel odd, but now . . . I recalled that time as if I'd been a different person. A foolish young girl. Recently rejected by my family and Connor, I'd been desperate for anyone who cared.

Good man though Clay was, we'd never been suited.

Not like . . .

My mind almost took me to the memory of first meeting Max at Charlene's wedding, the dance we'd shared, the spark of something that had thrilled me—but I snuffed it out.

Concern flickered across Charlene's face, and I followed her gaze to a woman staring—no, more like glaring—at me.

Her fair skin reminded me of smooth porcelain, her stillness of a statue. But her pink lips moved. Disdain tinged her low voice. "Are you happy now?"

I blinked. "Excuse me?"

"He was going to leave you." She leaned in and narrowed her eyes. "Is that why you killed him?"

Five

Heat rushed through me. I did my best to find my voice, but it came out slightly strangled. "Who are you?"

The woman straightened and cocked her chin. Her eyes glinted, bold despite the red rims, the smudged eyeliner. "I'm the one he loved."

I tried to ignore the acid filling my stomach.

Tried to keep my mind from spinning.

Just when I thought things couldn't get worse. Here came another blow. Another betrayal.

She stepped into my personal space. "You found out that night, didn't you?"

I smelled wine on her breath. "You should leave."

"No." She poked a finger at me. "You should. In handcuffs. I don't know how you fooled the cops, but they'll get evidence on you soon, and when they do—"

"Hey, what's going on here?" Dane stepped between us, head swiveling with concern. His gaze stopped on the woman. "Shelly, what are you doing?"

"Someone needs to give it to her straight instead of tiptoeing around her. We all know what she did."

Dane frowned, eyes darkening. He took her arm. "Come on—"

She stepped back and tried to shake him off. "Do you really believe her innocent act?" She scanned the room. "How can everyone be okay with her being here?" Tears fell onto her trembling chin. "Look at her. She doesn't even care that he's dead. She was a terrible wife. She—"

"Stop." Dane's jaw tensed. "Stop," he repeated, softer this time. He leaned closer to her. "You can't do this, Shelly. You've said enough. Let's go." He eased her away, and to my relief, she let him walk her out of the room.

I stood still, time ticking past.

Her existence shocked me, and yet . . . I should've known. All the extra hours Connor had claimed to work, yet money stayed tight.

How had he met her? Who was she? How long had this been going on?

Were there others?

The questions battered me, bruised me.

Sickness and anger swelled, engulfing me, smothering me.

"Hey." Charlene stepped to my side. I'd forgotten all about her. "I'm sorry." The expression on her face told me just how much. She appeared to search for the right thing to say. "She's just upset and taking it out on you."

Dane appeared beside me again. How had he rid himself of that woman so fast? His hand touched my shoulder, heavy with regret. "I'm sorry about that."

I looked at him and Charlene, both sorry, both concerned.

But Dane wasn't my friend. He was Connor's. I had to remember that. If Ian knew Connor tracked my phone, Dane probably did too. He'd never said a word. And now . . .

"You know that woman. You knew Connor was seeing her." I swallowed, surprised I felt almost as betrayed by Dane for not telling me. "How long?"

He paled slightly. "Brook—"

"Never mind. I'm done here." I turned. "Ella?" I scanned the people, spotted Ross, Connor's dad, but not Barb. I pushed through the crowd and located the small side room.

But no Ella.

Panic climbed my throat.

Charlene caught up to me. "Don't worry, kids like to wander. It'll be okay. We'll find her."

I raced back through the main room, my temples pulsing. I paused at Ross's side, interrupting his conversation, asking if he'd seen Ella.

He glanced around quickly before giving a short "No" and returning to his conversation about the time Connor had worked on a DeLorean.

I fumbled my way against the tide of people still filing into the funeral home, then burst out the double doors. "Ella!" I dashed into the lot and scanned the parked cars, turned to the side lot, and then the rear.

I spotted her climbing into the back seat of a familiar SUV.

"Ella, no! Stop!" I charged up to the vehicle.

The door swung shut, and Barb faced me, clearly perturbed. "Must you scream across the lot like that?"

My blood churned as I tried to reach past her. "What do you think you're doing with my daughter?"

"Relax, I was simply taking her out for some fresh air. It's all a bit too much for her here."

"You didn't even ask me." I threw open the door. "Ella."

She hesitated. "Am I in trouble?"

"No, sweetie, no." I pulled her close and out of the vehicle. "You didn't do anything wrong." Barb, however . . . I eyed her.

"Grandma said I was going to stay with them for a little while," Ella whispered.

Barb didn't deny it. In fact, she tilted her nose and stood firm, though she had the decency to look slightly chagrined. "You should think about it."

"She's my child," I said through clenched teeth. "She stays with me."

"She's our granddaughter." Barb laid a hand over her heart. "We only want what's best for her."

"I'm her mother. I'm what's best for her."

I could practically see Barb biting her tongue. "We'll have to come to some kind of agreement. Amicably, preferably, but it's up to you. Don't forget, Ross has associates in the courts." She lowered her voice. "You stole my son from me. You won't steal his daughter."

She walked away, heels clicking, as Charlene caught up to me.

My body trembled as I called after Barb, "You'll never take her from me. I won't let you." I lowered my voice and spoke to Charlene. "She can't, can she?" I smoothed Ella's hair, kissed her forehead, her cheeks, and squeezed her to me.

"I don't see how." But Charlene's tone revealed worry. Thanks to her overbearing grandfather, she was well acquainted with the problems money and power could bring.

My heart sank. Being free of Connor didn't make us free—not with his family setting their sights on us.

Charlene put her hand on my shoulder. "Let me take you home."

"No, that's okay. Thanks for coming, though. It means a lot to me. Truly."

"Mommy?" Ella tapped my arm. "What about ice cream? You promised, remember?"

Had I? Oh yes, days ago. This child did not forget. And she'd waited long enough. "You're right, Ella." I nodded. "Let's go get some."

Six

"I like your hair," Ella said, clearly in awe as she touched Charlene's shiny curls with sticky ice-cream fingers.

Charlene didn't pull away, just laughed. "You're so much gentler on my hair than my kids. I'm convinced they're trying to pluck me bald."

We sat in a vinyl booth with an excessive pile of brown paper napkins in front of us. Tension melted from my mind and shoulders much like our ice cream as we talked about old times.

Eventually, Charlene slid her dish aside. "Have you thought about moving back? To Creekside, I mean?"

Creekside. The town where I'd first met Connor. Still Charlene's town. "I don't know." I'd be closer to Charlene, but also not far from some of Connor's old friends. It would be too much like backtracking when I needed to move forward. Yet the thought of staying in Bloomington at the house where the bad memories outweighed the good . . . How wise was that?

I poked my spoon at the ice cream. "A fresh start would be nice. And I'd like to go back to school. I'd like to be a nurse someday." A labor and delivery nurse, if possible. I looked fondly at Ella working on her drippy cone. Not a day passed that I didn't marvel at her birth. Easily the best day of my life, despite the arduous labor.

And Charlene had been there, helping me through it. I could think of nothing more fulfilling than providing that kind of support for others.

Pointless dreams, Connor used to tell me. *Nurses have to be super smart.* The implication clear: he didn't think I had what it took.

A phone buzzed. Charlene glanced and silenced it. "Just Max. I'll call him back later."

Just Max. Such a simple, dismissive phrase. It didn't seem to fit him, at least not from what I recalled. In the relatively short time I'd known him, his energetic and magnetic personality had charmed me, and not because the world hailed him as a magnificent stage magician, but despite it.

Yet there was something almost magical about the way he'd made me feel that night we danced, my stomach twirling every time he spun me. When had I last felt that carefree?

He'd asked for my number before he flew home. Long phone conversations followed, and we'd become friends. I'd sensed there'd been the promise of something more... But he lived in California, and I in Wisconsin. Miles and worlds apart. And by the time he visited and officially asked me out, Connor had reentered my life, and I'd had to turn Max down.

It wasn't meant to be.

I gathered up the dirty napkins. "Well, it's getting late, and I should get this little lady home to bed. I'm sure she'll sleep well after that double-chocolate-fudge cone." I groaned.

"Not to brag, but I'm pretty good at telling bedtime stories." Charlene's eyes twinkled. "I'd be happy to lend a hand. Or in this case, my voice."

I paused on my way out of the booth. "But it's already late, and you have a long drive back."

She waved a hand. "I'm not driving back tonight. There's still the service tomorrow." Her voice lowered. "And burial."

She was staying for all of that? To be there for me? Emotion prickled the back of my eyes. "But where are you staying?"

"A hotel."

I shook my head. "We have plenty of room. You should stay with us." It came out a little too quickly. Stay in our house, where a murder occurred a week ago? What was I thinking? Even I didn't want to stay there. I couldn't expect—

"Sounds great, thanks."

Too relieved to reply, I nodded and dumped our garbage. We left the restaurant, and Charlene followed me to the house.

As my car crept up the driveway, my stomach knotted, distress mixing with the ice cream.

Faint porch light revealed the front door standing partially open.

My foot froze on the brake.

Was someone in my house?

I searched the shadows along the sides of the building, scanned the windows for movement or a stealthy silhouette. Not that I'd be able to see one with the lights off. Fear skittered through me. I couldn't go in there with possible danger lurking.

I put the car in park only halfway up the driveway.

"Mommy, why'd you stop?"

"Give me a second, hon." I hit the garage opener, half expecting someone to bolt out. Again, all appeared normal. But appearances could be deceiving.

And nothing felt normal.

Nothing felt safe.

I swallowed a lump and dialed the police.

* * *

By the time the authorities assured me the house and yard were all clear and I could enter, that was the last thing I wanted to do.

A great repulsion for this place filled me. All week I'd done my best to ignore it, jumping at the slightest noise or shadow. Not sleeping well.

Perhaps I'd forgotten to lock the door, the police suggested. The wind had blown it open. Happened all the time.

Maybe.

But maybe not.

The police escorted us inside before leaving, and I laid Ella, who'd fallen asleep in my arms, in her bed. I looked at her, so innocent and vulnerable. She trusted me with her life.

Charlene helped me lock the doors and turn on all the lights.

A murderer had entered my house once before. It could happen again.

The thought tortured me.

"I can't do it," I rasped. "I can't live here anymore. Not with Ella. I can't put her in danger."

Charlene nodded. "Come stay with us, as long as you want."

The kindness of her unhesitating offer filled me with gratitude.

But no.

For myriad reasons, no. Her house was the perfect size for her family. With us, it would be crowded. And I'd once dated Clay. As over him as I was, that would still be weird.

"Thank you, but I think I need to go someplace I've never lived before. A new town. So Ella and I can have a fresh start. Where no one knows about Connor or the murder." Where they wouldn't look at me with suspicion.

Where the murderer wouldn't find me.

Charlene nodded slowly. Her knotted brow smoothed and her eyes lit up. "We have a vacation home on the outskirts of a little town a few hours away. We don't use it in the winter. We will when the kids get older, but it's already paid for and just sitting there. It's perfect. Quiet and peaceful. No one will bother you."

It sounded tempting, but . . . "That's too much to ask."

"You didn't, I'm offering. No, insisting." She folded her arms. "Don't say you can't, because you can. And you should. Remember, you gave me a place to stay when I first moved to Creekside."

I almost laughed. "Under highly different circumstances." I'd admitted my selfish reason for that offer years ago, and I was still ashamed of it.

She grasped my hands. "You need to do this. For you and for Ella."

I thought for a long moment. My options were limited. Connor had left me with practically nothing in savings, and most of what our house would sell for would have to be used to pay back the bank. "Okay, as long as you let me pay rent." I'd get a job as soon as possible. Not that I was qualified for much or had any recent experience, since Connor hadn't let me work, but I'd do my best.

We talked late into the night, discussing details.

And so it was settled. After tomorrow's graveside service and funeral dinner, Ella and I would begin a new life in the small town of Vanishing Lakes.

The name sent a shiver through me, but in a good way.

What better place to disappear to?

Seven

"What does 'vanishing' mean, Mommy?" Ella asked from the back seat as we cruised the highway, heading for our new life. "Does it mean going really fast?"

I glanced at my speedometer and eased off the gas. Didn't need a ticket. "No, it means disappearing. Which means something goes away. Like . . . when clouds block the sun, your shadow disappears."

"Oh." Two beats of silence. "So are there lakes there or not?" Excitement touched her words. "Will we see them disappear?"

I laughed. "Yes, there are lakes. The house we're staying in will be on one of them." Mirror Lake, Charlene had said. "But no, they're not going to disappear."

"Then why is it called that?" I pictured her lower lip protruding in a pout.

"I don't know. Maybe long ago when people named the town, some lakes had dried up or something like that." I shrugged. "Or maybe someone just thought it was a good name."

"Mommy, I have another question."

Of course she did. She always did. Smiling, I lowered

the volume of the kids' songs playing through the car speakers.

"Did you kill Daddy?"

Alarm zinged through me. She couldn't have shocked me more if she'd slapped me.

"Of course not, Ella." I fought to keep my voice measured. "Why would you ask that?"

"Because that's what the other kids told me. At the dinner. They said that's what their parents said."

Anger flashed white across my vision. I pulled in a couple of deep breaths and focused on formulating a reply. I wanted names and numbers. Wanted to give those parents a piece of my mind. But that wouldn't do any good.

"I'm sorry they said that, sweetie. They shouldn't have." I clenched the wheel. "It isn't true. I would never, ever hurt your daddy."

"But he hurt you," she said in a small voice.

My heart squeezed. True, but that's not how I wanted her to remember him. "But he was nice most of the time." It wasn't a lie. To Ella, he was. "Remember when he used to give you piggyback rides? Or spin you around until you got dizzy?"

"I liked that." She sighed wistfully.

Taking her somewhere new was the right thing to do. I was convinced of that now more than ever.

"So why did they say you killed him?"

I exhaled slowly through my nose. "Sometimes people

say things because they don't know the truth. So they make up an answer even if it isn't the right one."

"So who *did* kill Daddy?"

A question no child should ever have to ask. "I don't know." I tried not to torture myself with the wondering. The last thing I wanted was for her to do so. Detective Bale had assured me they'd keep investigating, which included delving into Connor's background and questioning all his relatives, friends, coworkers, and acquaintances. That included Shelly, Dane, and Ian. Even his parents.

As I well knew, anyone who had any contact with Connor could be a suspect. But then again, if the culprit was a stranger, where did that leave us?

I didn't want suspicion consuming our lives. And certainly not Ella's. "The police are trying to find out. It's their job." Not mine.

"But what if they don't?"

"Then they don't."

"But I want to know."

I adjusted my hold on the wheel. "Some things only God knows, sweetie. We may not like it, but that's just the way it is."

"That's stupid." She kicked my seat.

"Ella," I said sharply. "Don't kick the seat. And you know I don't want you using that word. It's not nice." A dull headache started at the base of my skull, but I turned up the kids' songs, hoping to redirect Ella's attention.

A little while later, snowflakes dotted the windshield, and I flicked on the wipers. The steady snowfall frosted the trees and grass beautifully but soon turned the road slick, forcing me to slow. And we'd already been driving too long for a restless six-year-old.

An hour later, I assured Ella, as much as myself, "We're almost there."

"But how will you find it? It's so dark."

"I have the directions on my phone." My new phone, with a new number. No one had it but those I wanted to. Charlene and the police. "It shows me where to go."

"What if I don't like living there?" Ella said in a small voice.

I bit my lip. "But you will. Look, we're heading into town now. Just look at this cute place." Ornate street-lamps illuminated the snow in halos as we passed a row of old-fashioned storefronts. I caught a couple of names. FlapJack's Diner. Early Riser Bakery. I spotted a grocery store, then pointed out a library.

I enjoyed the quick tour, especially since I didn't plan to come to town often. We passed one lake, then another, the open expanses stretching into darkness. A rambling road took us through snow-cloaked trees. No streetlights here.

No houses, either.

But according to my phone, there were only a few more turns. I slowed to a careful crawl on a swooping curve, then continued through more wooded terrain. I paused at what appeared to be a driveway, then saw it led to a small parking area. A sign revealed it to be a public-access lot for Mirror Lake.

We were very close now. A minute later, I squinted at the numbers on a metal sign illuminated by my head-lights.

"Here we are." Good thing the driveway was flat, or I wouldn't make it up the snowy surface. Wind swirled more flakes across our path as the dark house came into view. Bigger than I'd pictured. Much bigger.

I'd expected a cute little cottage, a modest home at most.

This place stretched generously across the lot and included a full attached garage. Nothing temporary about it. It could easily be a very comfortable year-long res-idence.

For the first time, I questioned how Charlene and Clay could afford this. I knew his carpentry business had taken off, but still. Had he built all this? It was bigger than their current home. But then, Charlene did come from a wealthy family . . .

Again I was touched by just how much she had done for me. For us.

I pulled into the garage. Ella yawned as I helped her out. After not sleeping a wink the entire ride, now she was tired. Which was just as well. The emotionally draining week had us both exhausted.

Falling into a safe, warm bed sounded heavenly. And

if the mattress and sheets were anything like the rest of this place, they would be quality. The entryway—larger than my dining room—flowed into a high-ceilinged living room with almond-colored walls. A large fireplace drew my gaze. I made sure we pulled off our boots before stepping off the rug and onto the polished wood floors.

Sleep called to me. After switching on the main breaker and gas according to Charlene's instructions, and a cursory check of all doors and windows—so many windows—to ensure they were locked, I turned up the heat and retreated to the master bedroom.

While I was glad I'd promised to pay rent, the sum we'd agreed upon sounded paltry now, a fraction of this place's actual worth. And I didn't even have a job lined up.

But that was a concern for another day. We brushed our teeth, changed into pajamas, said our prayers, and nestled into bed.

* * *

I wasn't sure what woke me, but my mind went from bleary to alert in an instant. Years of living with Connor had conditioned me to snap to attention at the slightest noise.

Ella's breathing remained steady. Warm air hummed from the furnace.

Thump. Thump.
Thump.

Distinct, heavy footsteps.

My body went rigid. My heart rate surged.

I wanted to bury my head under the blankets and pretend I'd heard nothing. Like a coward.

But I couldn't be a coward. I had to protect Ella.

Praying she'd stay asleep, I felt for my phone on the bedside table. Not there. I racked my brain, almost groaning when I realized I'd left it charging in the kitchen.

I slid from the covers, already missing their false sense of safety. My bare feet touched icy floor.

Heartbeat thudding in my ears, I crept to the door and eased it open, then slid along the wall to the kitchen. Plenty of shadows to hide in.

Across the way, a dark figure moved. A man.

A scream caught in my throat.

He set something down. Rummaged through something. Straightened. Stilled.

Could he see me?

Hands clammy, I felt along the cold granite countertop for my phone. Almost there. Fingers inched until I touched it, seized it.

The screen turned on. Too bright.

I pulled it close, attempting to shield the glow with my body.

Too late.

"Who's there?" The man's deep voice filled me with alarm as he headed my way.

Eight

Terror bound my tongue. My hand scrambled for something to defend myself with. Kitchen block. Knives.

I seized one and wielded the large blade at the approaching figure. "Stop. Stay back!"

Lights burst on, flooding the room and smarting my eyes. I blinked. Blood roared in my ears. I brandished the knife.

The man drew back. His startled expression changed to disbelief. "Brook?"

The knife shook in my hand. Relief washed through me, replacing fear, but still unnerving me. My overwrought mind and adrenaline-saturated muscles couldn't handle this.

"Max?" I could no more believe he was here than I could believe in magic. Yet he stood right in front of me. "What are you doing here?"

Something like amusement flickered across his face, then died. "Not trying to get stabbed." He held up his hands. "Mind putting that away?"

I blinked at the glinting blade, horrified. What if he

hadn't turned on the lights in time?

Concern overtook his features with a seriousness that further unsettled me. "Sorry I scared you. I saw the car but assumed Charlene was here with the family."

My shoulders sagged. I lowered the knife to the counter and released it, then clasped my hands together to steady them. "I'm sorry. I-I didn't know anyone else was coming here. So when I heard footsteps . . . I'm a light sleeper." Had to be. Threats could come when least expected. I shivered, swallowed. Wished the knife would disappear. "I'm so sorry."

"It's okay, just a misunderstanding." Max stepped back. "You look cold. Why don't you sit down?" He nodded toward the living room. "I'll light a fire." He turned, then turned again, like maybe he didn't trust having his back to me.

Couldn't blame him for that.

I shuddered, rubbed my arms, and nodded. Stepping forward, I passed a suitcase and a duffel bag. In the living room, I settled into a gray suede sectional. If I didn't know better, I could almost believe this was a dream. As if my recent thoughts of Max had conjured him up.

He kept glancing at me as he arranged logs. What a sight I must be with my shell-shocked eyes, pillow-mussed hair, and wrinkly pajama sweats.

He, on the other hand, looked good in his simple black slacks and fitted button shirt. Better than good. More man now than boy. His hair was just long enough to curl, something Charlene had once told me he hated. He must have gotten over that. It suited him. He wasn't tall enough to tower over me, but his athletic build and strong facial features made him seem almost imposing. Confident. And something about that was comforting.

Realizing I was staring, I averted my eyes.

"That oughta do it." He brushed off his hands and stood. "Nothing like a fire in the middle of a blizzard." He dropped into a chair. "So why don't you tell me how you ended up here?" The corner of his mouth stretched. "Since I'm pretty sure you didn't break and enter, I'm guessing my sister had something to do with this."

I nodded. "I needed somewhere to stay, and she said this place doesn't get used in the winter." Uneasiness prodded at me. Charlene had seemed pleased when Max and I became friends years ago, but she wouldn't purposely push us back together like this, would she? No, that wouldn't be like her. This had to be an honest mistake.

"Always overgenerous, that sister of mine." Was that a thread of irritation in his voice?

I tried to tuck my bare feet out of sight. "She never mentioned you were coming."

"Because she didn't know. This was a spur-of-the-moment trip. Didn't think I had to check with her." He scrubbed a hand over his jaw. "She's always saying it's too far to go with the kids, and why come in the dead of winter? Biggest attraction here's the lakes, so unless you like ice fishing . . ."

He glanced around. "Anyway, how long were you planning on staying?"

The casual expectation in his voice was clear. He hoped I was leaving as soon as possible. I swallowed. If he wanted the place, what right did I have to it? Not like I'd signed a lease. I should probably call Charlene. But not this time of night. When had he last spoken to her? Did he know anything about my situation? And if he did, would it change anything?

Disappointment touched me. For a second, when he'd invited me to sit, I'd had a ridiculous image of us chatting comfortably, catching up in front of the cozy fire as if we could pick up at that sweet spot from long ago.

Instead, Max had cut right to the point, not even a *How have you been?* But then, would I really want to answer that?

His keen green eyes didn't hold welcome or warmth. Only a steady inquisitiveness, and perhaps a touch of impatience. He'd likely come all the way from California. Had to be tired.

"I can leave tomorrow." I didn't know where I'd go, but I'd figure something out. "It's no problem," I heard myself say.

Satisfaction settled over his face, as if he'd expected nothing less. A man used to getting his way.

"Well, this blizzard might make tomorrow a little tricky, so don't feel like you have to rush out first thing," he said indulgently. He leaned forward as if about to stand. "You in the guest room downstairs, or did you take the master?"

Heat unrelated to the fire swept over me. Did he have to phrase it that way? Why would I have gone to the basement? Yet admitting to taking the grandest room suddenly made me feel ashamed. Presumptuous.

I stood. "I'm sorry, we can move to the basement."

"We?"

"Mommy!"

At Ella's terrified shriek, I forgot all about Max and flew to the bedroom, practically skidding across the floor.

"It's okay. I'm here, Ella, I'm here. You're okay, don't worry." I flicked on a light, pulled her into my arms, and wiped damp hair from her hot forehead as she whimpered against my chest. I rocked her, hummed to her, pressed my cheek to hers.

Too much drama in her life, too many changes, and now tomorrow another one. I held her till she and my arms fell asleep, then eased her back down. "I'll be right back," I whispered, my arms tingling as the circulation returned.

I doubted Max was still waiting. We'd have plenty of time to finish the awkward conversation tomorrow, but I'd check, so as not to appear any ruder than I already had.

Only a dim light remained on in the kitchen. I spied a large twelve-pack of beef ramen noodles on the floor near the counter. The fire still flickered, though barely. I was about to turn when I heard Max's voice rise, clearly irritated.

Stepping forward, I heard his words fly up from the basement. No door sealed the stairs off. There was just an open landing and iron rails. "Would've been nice if you'd given me a heads up, Char."

A pause, then, "Yeah, well I've been busy. You know how many messages I got today? And just 'cause I said use it whenever—I still get a say. I still own it. So I think—"

He owned the place? I pressed a hand to my head. Oh, this just kept getting better. And I hated causing bitter words between him and Charlene.

"Not everyone has to be our charity case. I'm sure she can—"

My ears burned.

"No, I didn't get the chance. This is a huge inconvenience. I don't want to be cooped up with her and her screaming kid. That's the last thing I need right now—"

I'd heard enough. My humiliation turned to anger. What had happened to the kind, considerate young man of five years ago? Or had it all been an act? He was a stage performer, after all.

I practically stomped back to my room, sure Max wouldn't even hear. This fancy place was probably too well insulated.

I peered out my window. Wild wind drove sheets of snow into the dark. Ella and I certainly wouldn't stay where we weren't welcome. And the last thing we needed was an angry man anywhere near us.

Much as my body craved rest, I was too upset to fall asleep. I lay in bed stewing, and soon after the first signs of gray morning light, I grabbed our few bags, roused Ella, donned our coats, and settled back into the car.

I breathed on my fingers to warm them while the car heated, then backed out through the thick accumulation of snow and saw, to my dismay, plenty of flakes still falling.

Ella moaned. "Why are we driving *again*?"

"Hush, dear. Go back to sleep." I pressed the gas and the tires turned, barely gripping the driveway. I muttered. Why couldn't something go right? Sometimes I wondered if all the bad things that happened to me were God's punishment for all the poor choices I'd made. I knew I shouldn't think that way, but at times like this, the evidence seemed overwhelming.

No sooner did I reach the road than I had to navigate a tricky curve. Just when I thought we'd made it, the back of the car slipped. I cranked the wheel, overcorrecting. We slid again.

Right off the side of the road.

The car tilted. Halted.

I tried driving forward, then reversing. Engine revved. Tires spun. But we didn't move.

We were stuck firmly in the ditch.

Nine

"What happened, Mommy? Why's the car leaning funny?"

I shook my head. We were barely out of sight of Max's driveway.

"This isn't fun." Ella huffed. "Let's go back. I've gotta go potty."

Of course.

Holding in a frustrated laugh, I unbuckled and ducked out the door. "Come on." I scooped her from her seat and struggled to carry her as I waded through the snow, knee-high in some places.

The driveway seemed at least twice as long when walking—and with Ella wiggling a potty dance in my arms.

"Almost there." I hauled in a breath.

Only a few more steps to the door.

Ella squirmed. My foot met a slick spot, and I slipped. Tumbled.

My head plunked into snow and connected with something rock-hard. Pain burst through my skull. With a whimper to match Ella's, I shuddered and blacked out.

* * *

I'd done something I shouldn't. Taken the car without permission. Connor would be angry.

There'd be hell to pay.

Cracking my eyes weakly, I spotted a figure beside me and groaned. He was here. He'd found me.

Sharp pain forced my eyes closed. If I pretended to sleep, maybe he'd leave. I needed some time to brace myself for what was sure to come.

Or maybe he'd already retaliated. Yes, wasn't that why my head hurt?

"Brook, can you hear me?"

His voice could be so gentle when he chose, but I wasn't fooled.

"I'm sorry."

Sure he was. So predictable, this man, and yet . . . not.

"I didn't mean you had to leave today." A sigh. "I was a jerk. I admit it."

Wait. Admitting fault? Contrite as he could act, the fault was still always mine. No, this couldn't be Connor. Then who . . . ?

Curiosity inched my eyes back open.

Max.

My pulse settled slightly, then picked up in a different way. Max. After all these years . . . I never thought I'd see him again.

Safe, warm assurance slid through my limbs, until I

recalled his harsh words. My morning retreat. Ella.

I shot up. My gaze darted around the room, then back to him. "Where's Ella? Is she okay?"

His eyebrows rose. "Yeah, she's fine, don't worry. She's watching TV in the living room. You're the one who's hurt. You hit your head on the front step. Luckily she was smart enough to pound on the door and yell till I heard her." He looked momentarily chagrined. "Waking me up isn't easy. That girl's got some lung power."

A short, relieved laugh escaped me, and I sank back onto the pillow. "Yes, yes she does." Got it from her dad.

My smile faded.

I reached up to find a thick bandage cushioning a tender lump on my forehead and winced.

Max leaned forward in his chair, elbows on his knees. "You didn't have to run off at the crack of dawn like that."

I met his gaze. "I never would have stayed here if I knew this place belonged to you."

"Ouch." He leaned back. "You sure know how to hurt a guy's ego."

I was fairly certain his ego could handle it.

He pressed his lips together into a disapproving line. "But I deserved that. You overheard me, didn't you?"

"At that volume? Hard not to. And did you really wake Charlene up in the middle of the night just to yell at her? She has kids. She needs every second of sleep she can get."

He waved a hand like it was no big deal. "She wouldn't have answered if she didn't want to. She loves hearing from me. She understands I've got a crazy schedule."

"Well, it sounds like it wouldn't hurt for you to be a bit more considerate."

He eyed me like he didn't agree but would let it go. For now. "I'm sorry for what you overheard."

Meaning he wasn't sorry for what he'd said?

But I wouldn't bother clarifying.

I'd heard plenty of apologies in my life, and they didn't mean much to me anymore. They were too easy to give, too easy to fake.

Max sighed and dragged a hand down his face. "I was overtired. And dealing with some stuff. Still, not an excuse."

I'd also heard a lot of justifications. Even so, I did owe him some gratitude. "Thanks for bringing us inside. And"—I pointed to my forehead—"for this."

"How do you feel?"

"Like I smashed my head." The pain ranked up there with one of the headaches Connor had given me.

He nodded. "Let's hope it's not a concussion. I got a few of those from snowboarding back in the day. Back when it wasn't cool to wear a helmet," he added with a touch of wistfulness, like he wouldn't mind experiencing that risk again. "Let me know if you feel nauseous or anything. I can take you somewhere to get checked out."

"I'm sure I'm fine. It's just a bad headache." Nothing

I hadn't pushed through before.

He leaned close, then closer, eyes intent, making my heart palpitate. If I didn't know better, I'd think he was about to kiss me.

My voice came out panicky. "What are you doing?"

"Looking at your pupils." He said it as if it were obvious. "Seeing if one's dilated more than the other. Sign of a concussion." He leaned back. "Looks good, but there's some water and Tylenol if you want it." He pointed to the bedside table.

"Thanks." I was especially thankful he didn't know my brain was oddly hung up on the kiss that hadn't happened. My head really was messed up.

He stood. "You hungry?"

I realized I was. "A little."

"Okay." He turned. "I'll be right back."

"Can you tell Ella to come in?" I didn't like her out of my sight for long.

"Yeah, sure."

She scampered in with a big grin. "I saved you, Mommy."

I squeezed her. "You sure did, baby. Thank you." I kissed her nose.

She patted my cheeks. "Your friend Max is nice. How come if he's your friend you never told me about him?"

My friend. Had he told her that?

"Sometimes friends drift apart." And sometimes they're forced apart. "I haven't seen him since you were one."

"I like him. And he's strong. He picked you up and carried you in here."

"Hey." I tweaked her nose playfully. "Just how heavy do you think I am?"

She giggled, though I doubted she understood my humor.

She poked gently at my bandage. "Does it hurt?"

"Not much now that it's all patched up."

"It was so icky and gushing blood."

Given that she thought a pinprick of redness was a reason to scream, I figured my wound wasn't all that bad.

"Max let me watch him clean it, and I helped put on the giant Band-Aid. Maybe I could be a nurse someday too."

She was referring to me, eager to follow in my footsteps in a dream I hadn't even begun to make happen. The confidence of a child was a beautiful thing.

"Of course you can, Ella. I'm so proud of you."

"Max said you were going to be okay and you just needed some rest, and then he made me noodly soup for breakfast. It was good."

"Let's hope your mom likes it as much as you do." Max appeared with a steaming bowl on a tray and handed it to me. "If I'd known I had guests, I would've brought some better food. When the snow lets up and the roads clear, I'll get some real groceries. And get your car towed out."

I lifted a spoonful and sipped the hot broth. "Don't go to any trouble. I'll take care of it and be out of your way soon."

"Listen, about that." Max hauled a chair close and straddled it. "First off, you need to get better. A few days at least. And after that"—he spread his hands—"you can stay as long as you want."

He glanced at Ella, lowered his voice, and met my eyes. "If I'd had any idea of everything you'd been through, I never would've tried to send you away."

Everything I'd been through. How much had Charlene shared? How much did she know and how much had she guessed?

It couldn't have been much more than that my husband was killed and his family thought I was responsible. And that they wanted to take Ella from me.

Which was more than enough.

Feeling exposed, I avoided his gaze. But even Charlene didn't know about the abuse. So I could rest assured he didn't know either.

Relaxing slightly, I blew on the broth, more of a sigh than anything. "Thank you, but we don't need charity. It would be better if we went to a motel until I find another place." I tried not to think about how rapidly that would drain our meager funds. And as long as the murder investigation was going on, the life insurance money would be hung up indefinitely.

"But I like it here," Ella piped up. "It's big and fancy

and the TV is *huge*." She stretched her arms as far as they could go and stood on her tiptoes. "Even bigger than this!"

Max chuckled. "She's got good taste. That's one of my favorite things about this place too."

"We'd be in your way." I stirred the noodles. I'd distinctly heard how he felt about us staying, and the only thing that had changed was his sympathy. And I didn't want sympathy.

"And Ella is anything but quiet. We'd interfere with your work." Now I was assuming. Was he here to work? And if so, what did that even mean? Practice tricks? Develop new ones? Or was he simply on vacation, planning to do some of that ice fishing he'd mentioned? Either way, he hadn't expected us to be here.

"She's fine," he said, "and she's right, this place is huge. You wouldn't be in the way. The downstairs is more than enough for me."

Hadn't sounded that way last night.

"It's got everything, bedroom, bathroom, work space, even a little kitchen. Besides, an agreement's an agreement, and Charlene told me you already paid a month's rent." He shrugged. "And I'm not giving it back."

As if that paltry sum could mean anything to him.

"Let's vote. That's what we do in school." Ella danced around the room. "I vote to stay here." She raised her hand.

Max raised his, grin matching hers. "Come on, can't argue with logic like that."

I could, but my aching head stopped me. "We'll take it one day at a time," I said cautiously. "That's all I can promise."

Ten

I wasn't stupid. Of course Charlene had sweet-talked Max into making us stay.

So his asking us to shouldn't make me feel this good. As if he truly wanted us here.

Such thoughts deserved no attention, just like the ones that had occasionally slipped into my mind over the past years. What if our timing had been different? What if I'd stayed strong and not given in to Connor telling me I needed him, that Ella needed him, and that marrying him was the right thing to do?

No amount of regret changed the fact that I'd made my vow and believed marriage was till death.

Now that death had come, I shouldn't feel so relieved. Guilt pricked, and I told myself sternly this was no silly fantasy, no second chance at a relationship. I rubbed my temples. Hitting my head had really done a number on me.

Over the years, I'd resisted the occasional urge to look Max up online and catch up on his life. I had no good reason to, only a strange curiosity. What's more, if Connor had ever checked my browsing history—which

he occasionally did—and seen such a search, the reper-
cussions would've been terrible.

Though it almost felt wrong now, I made myself ask,
"So how's your career going? Still the world's top stage
magician?"

Max made a dismissive sound. "Life in the limelight's
overrated."

"You're a magician?" Ella's eyes sparked with excitement. "Where's your rabbit? Magicians always have
rabbits—they pull them out of hats." She waited one
second. "And where's your hat?" Her eyes narrowed.
"You don't look like a magician."

Max cocked an eyebrow. "Maybe that's my plan—
trick you into thinking I'm not, so that when you least
expect it, I can surprise you."

With a flick of his hand, he produced a bright red
handkerchief, then leaned forward to offer it to Ella,
whose smile stretched bigger than I'd seen since we'd
stopped for ice cream. She grabbed it with a happy
squeal—and out sailed a line of handkerchiefs knotted
together in one long, flowing rainbow of colors.

"Ooh!" Ella laughed, so delighted that she jumped up
and down. "Do more! Do more!"

I lifted a warning finger at Max. "Number one rule
when it comes to kids—don't start something fun unless
you want to do it forever." Only half joking, I eyed Ella.
"I'm sure Mr. Perigard has other things to do, so let's
leave him be. Why don't you unpack your coloring books

and markers and come up here next to me?" I patted the bed.

"That's boring."

Her words stunned me. She never turned down an opportunity to color with me.

"I want to see more tricks."

"I don't mind." Max sounded genuine. "My favorite thing about performing has always been entertaining people, and her reaction's the best. Tell you what." He crouched beside Ella. "Give me a little time to get ready, and I'll put on a show for you. How's that sound?"

"Yay!"

"Nothing scary," I added. Surely he had the sense to know that cutting a person in half would not be an appropriate trick.

"As long as you promise I'm not gonna hear any more of that 'Mr. Perigard.'" He gave a mock shudder. "Not from you or Ella."

"But it's the respectful way for a child to address you."

"Sure, if I were my grandfather. Which, thank the Lord, I'm not."

His grandfather. Right. From what little I'd seen of the eccentric man at Charlene's wedding, I couldn't blame Max for his aversion. "Okay, if you feel that strongly about it."

"Oh, I do."

Less than twenty minutes later, Ella sat in my lap as we delighted in an array of mind-bending illusions. Max began with a few clever card tricks, made coins vanish and reappear behind Ella's ears, then moved on to deftly manipulating metal rings so that they passed through each other and linked. He cut a rope in two, tied the pieces together, then slid the knot right off, leaving the same long length of rope he'd started with.

We looked on in wonder and clapped enthusiastically when he swept a final bow.

"How did you get your magic?" Ella bounced up from my lap. "If I pray real hard, do you think God will give me magic?"

I opened my mouth, ready to launch into a long-winded lecture of everything wrong with that statement, when Max chuckled.

"People call it magic, but it's really just clever tricks of the eye or hand. God's already given you what you need for that—a brain." He rifled a deck of cards in a seamless stream from one hand to the next, like a flowing bridge. "With lots of practice, you can make impossible things look possible, but there's a logical explanation behind each trick."

"Okay . . ." Ella's brow puckered. "So how do you do your tricks?"

"Ah, but there's a saying in this business—a good magician never reveals his secrets. Because once you know, it's not nearly as fun." Something odd flickered in his eyes—gone so quickly, maybe I'd imagined it.

He turned and began packing his props. "Time to let

you get some rest." He nodded my way. "I'll be downstairs. Just text or call if you need anything." We exchanged numbers and he left.

Ella chattered on about the tricks. "I want him to teach me how to do them all."

"That was very nice of him to put on a show, but I don't want you begging or bothering him, understand? He's a very busy man."

While Ella began coloring, I couldn't resist pulling out my phone and starting an internet search, feeling slightly guilty. But if I was staying here even for just a day or two, a simple search was not uncalled for.

After weeding out articles about the other Maxwell Perigards—Max's grandfather and father—I found plenty to keep me reading.

Of course there were accounts from his teen years of the famous kidnapping. Charlene had shared some of that story with me, though she didn't like to speak of it.

The articles that most caught my attention were the ones from the last day or two.

Shows canceled, fans irate. Max's longtime assistant, a stunning beauty with flaming red hair, had left him amid a flurry of outrage. Sources blamed Max's out-of-control drinking and volatile moods and temper. Witnesses claimed he'd blown up at her, threatened her.

I couldn't believe it. I didn't want to keep reading, but I had to.

Headline after headline.

Max Perigard's Relationship With Assistant Goes Up in Smoke.

Perigard's Sensational Rise to Fame Followed by Sudden Fall From Favor: Is This the End of His Career?

Perigard's Greatest Secrets Exposed.

Last Act? Max Perigard Disappears. No One's Seen Him in Days.

My head swam and my stomach swirled with sudden nausea.

If any of these reports could be relied upon—and some of these sites were likely no better than online tabloids—I was surprised Max didn't appear more stressed.

But of course, he could act.

He was famous for deception, after all.

But Max as a belligerent, violent-tempered drunk? That didn't sound like the man who'd just helped me, the man I'd known years ago, or the brother Charlene spoke so kindly of. Was there another side to him I'd never glimpsed?

People weren't always what they seemed. I knew that better than most. Was I wrong to stay here even for a short time?

Despite my head flashing with pain, I clicked on an accompanying video and saw a performance clip from last year. As soon as the sound kicked in, Ella's head popped up from her coloring book. She watched as Max made a red sports car disappear on stage, then reappear.

"Cool! Let's watch more!"

I turned off my phone.

"Hey!"

"Enough screen time for us today." I tucked the phone away, but it wasn't as easy to tuck away my unsettling concerns.

Ella and I needed obscurity, peace, and healing. Not more problems.

Maybe that's what Max had come here for as well, to regroup and escape the public eye. But if so, how long could it last?

Neither one of us needed the drama associated with the other.

And most disturbing of all—even in scandalous rumors, there were often grains of truth.

My injury and lack of money aside, if I discovered even the slightest indication of a dark side lingering beneath Max's charming exterior, we'd have to go.

Eleven

"Mommy was watching you on her phone."

I forced my ramen noodles down and almost swallowed wrong. Why did Ella have to word it that way?

We were sitting around the dining table that evening, having a quiet, simple meal until she piped up with that.

"Oh?" Max looked inordinately pleased with himself.

I had to say something to keep him from getting the wrong idea. "It was just a short video. Ella wanted to see more of your tricks."

"But Mommy wouldn't let me."

Max's amused gaze bounced from me to Ella. "Did you see this one? My greatest trick of all." Solemnly, he proceeded to set his spoon on his nose, then removed his hand and let the silverware dangle from his face.

Ella cracked up into such a fit of giggles that she rolled out of her chair.

I pursed my lips and fought to keep a straight face.

"Come on." Max pointed my way, spoon still hanging. "You know you want to smile."

A laugh escaped me, and Ella hopped back onto her seat. "Can you teach me that one?"

He plucked the spoon from his nose and aimed it at her. "You bet."

"Lovely." I dabbed my mouth with my napkin. "I look forward to getting a call from school about that one."

"When am I going back to school?" Ella asked. "It's been forever."

Her "forever" was—I counted—eight days. Granted, a lot had occurred during that time. Our lives had changed completely. The stable normality of school would probably be good for her, yet I worried about it as Max demonstrated how to do the spoon trick—something about rubbing it against the tip of his nose a certain way.

I couldn't keep Ella from school forever, no matter how much I wanted to keep her in sight. But she might not realize that returning to school meant starting at a different one, and I didn't relish explaining that she'd have to make new friends. At this age, it should be easy for her. But it would be yet another change she'd have to deal with.

"Look, Mommy!" When she spoke, the spoon fell from her nose. "But I had it, I did!"

"You did," Max agreed, and eyed me. "She did."

As we cleared the table after dinner and Ella played with her dolls on the living room rug, he said, "I hope you don't mind that I taught her that."

"Oh." I waved my hand. "Of course not. It's good fun. She needs that."

"Right? What kid doesn't? Char gets all bent out of shape when I try to show her kids stuff like that, thinks I'm turning them into bad-mannered barbarians or something."

I swallowed a small laugh. Charlene could be a touch too exacting at times.

Max turned on the faucet and rinsed his bowl. "So now that the snow's tapering off, I'll grab some groceries tomorrow. Anything in particular you want me to get? I'm guessing not more ramen?"

I shook my head. "You really like it that much?"

He shrugged. "What I like is that it's easy. Back home in California, I eat a lot of takeout, but that's not much of an option way out here. Especially not during a blizzard." He plugged the drain and squirted in too much soap. "Who's got time for cooking?"

Me. Every day for the past four years. Rain or shine, pain or fine. I smiled as I emptied Ella's unfinished food into the trash. "I guess it depends how busy you are."

He nodded. "I love being busy, just not boring everyday-chores kind of busy. Creative busy. Being free to focus with no distractions, no interruptions—"

"Mommy, come and watch. My dolls are putting on a dance show!"

"Like that?" But I smiled so he'd know I was joking. Sort of. My life was only everyday kind of busy.

Our lives were worlds apart.

"Max," Ella called, "you can watch too."

He took a step, but I stopped him with my hand. "Don't feel like you have to."

"Hey, she put up with my performance." He cracked a smile. "Anyway, I'm on vacation." A muscle flickered in his jaw, and his grin faded. "I've gotta learn to not be so busy."

It felt like an opening, where I could mention my concern over what I'd read online, but I didn't know how to phrase it without making it sound like an accusation.

Then Ella started her show, and my opportunity was lost.

* * *

I'd just gotten Ella settled into bed when a tap sounded on the door. I unlocked and opened it to find Max standing there.

"So I thought I should warn you, I should probably wake you up once tonight, just to be safe. Because of your possible concussion. Char used to insist on doing that for me." He scratched his chin. "She was smart about that kind of stuff. So it's probably a good idea. If you're okay with it."

Really? It seemed excessive. But also . . . oddly nice for someone to care that much.

"I mean, your brain could have internal bleeding and we might not catch it in time. This way, if you don't wake up, I'll know to call an ambulance."

"Right. Very comforting." I glanced back at Ella,

thankful she was asleep and hadn't overheard. "It's up to you."

"Okay then. I'll set an alarm. Char would kill me if I let something happen to you." He pulled out his phone and walked away. "Good night."

* * *

A whisper. A man's voice.

Connor?

Please, no.

I lurched awake.

"Hey, Brook, easy. It's just me, Max." He stepped back. "How do you feel? How's your head?"

"Fine. It's fine." Morning light framed the edges of the window shade and painted Max as a grayish silhouette.

"Sorry I didn't check in earlier." He rubbed his hair. "I must've slept through my alarm or turned it off in my sleep. I've been known to do that. Glad you're okay." He headed for the door. "It's still really early, so go back to sleep if you want."

My muscles gladly relaxed. Ella still lay curled beside me, so I closed my eyes.

Before dropping off, an unsettling thought flickered through my groggy head. Good thing my life hadn't depended on Max, because he probably would've been too late.

* * *

Ella nudged me awake. "Max is out playing in the snow. Can we go play too?"

Huh? I kept my eyes closed, yearning for just one more minute of oblivious rest. But my mind was already activated. Had I heard her right?

"Give me a second to wake up, sweetie." A moment later, I forced myself out of bed, then padded to the bathroom and splashed water on my face. The chill invigorated my skin and cleared my vision. I removed the bandage from my forehead and decided it could stay off.

I changed into presentable clothes and followed Ella to the front door, where she pointed out the window.

"Oh, honey, he's just shoveling the driveway. That's not fun, it's a lot of work." I paused, my gaze lingering on his strong form hefting shovel loads like they were nothing. Not that I could see muscles beneath the bulk of his coat, but I pictured them anyway.

Realizing that, I turned and headed into the kitchen and started coffee. Tried not to be stunned by the beauty of the view in the daylight. The deck faced the lake and would be amazing to relax on in the summer. But right now, staying snuggled in warmth sounded so much better than wading through snow.

Max stomped inside and brushed snow from his pants. "Hey, good morning. I'm heading out for those groceries now." He grabbed a scarf and wound it around his neck and lower half of his face. Odd that he was doing that now after he'd already been out in the cold. When he popped on a baseball cap and a pair of sunglasses, I couldn't even tell it was him.

And that, I realized, was the point.

"Hiding from your fans?" I regretted the question the moment it was out. After what I'd learned, this was likely a sore spot. I couldn't read any reaction behind his cover, but quickly added, "You don't have to go. I could do the shopping."

"No, stay and rest."

My head felt okay, but I didn't argue. Living with Connor, I'd learned which battles were worth choosing. My heart plummeted at the realization that my mind still worked that way. I needed to purge his influence from my decision-making.

Ella looked up from the sleeve of crackers she was munching. "You have a big hill in your backyard. Do you have any sleds?"

"Sorry, kid, I don't."

I faced her. "Why don't you go use your watercolors?" When she moved to get them, I lowered my voice. "She's getting cabin fever. Not that this is a cabin—this place is so big." I doubted he'd taken it as an insult, so why was I tripping over my words? "I just mean I'm going to have to take her out to get some exercise soon. But the temperature, brrr." I rubbed my arms. "Maybe this afternoon when it's a little warmer, and I use that term loosely."

"I don't blame her. I hate being cooped up too."

After Max left and Ella tired of painting, I put cartoons on for her. I sipped my coffee and gazed out the large picture window. Snow swooshed across the backyard in a lively swirl of powder. A few large evergreens dotted the hill, which swept down to the frozen lake. Stark trees rimmed the shoreline, their branches heavy with snow.

My gaze followed the shoreline a ways, and I could just make out the side of a little cottage with one window peeking through the trees. The only other sign of possible human life.

The cartoons didn't hold my attention as they did Ella's, and I realized this was a good time to call Charlene.

When she didn't answer, I brought up my email and scanned the messages. What was this? I leaned forward in my chair. My fingers tightened on my phone. No, it couldn't be. My blood ran cold.

Someone was messing with me.

Had to be.

Because I had a message from Connor.

Twelve

Sometime later, the garage door opened and I heard Max hauling groceries into the kitchen.

I should help him.

But I remained glued to my chair, sickness churning the bitter coffee in my stomach.

"So look what I found." Max appeared in the entryway looking pleased with himself and holding two bright plastic sleds.

Ella shrieked with delight and raced over to them.

I blinked, barely processing the scene, as if seeing it from a distance through a hazy lens.

Max's brow dipped. Still wearing boots, he set the sleds down and crossed to my side. "Hey, what's wrong? Is your headache back? Do you feel sick?"

He reached out as if to feel my forehead, but I jerked away.

He froze. Something dark and disconcerting crossed his face.

"I'm sorry. I just . . ." I shook my head. I was vaguely aware of Ella sitting in first one sled, then the other. I lowered my voice. "I got an email. From Connor, my husband." My dead husband. "I mean, it came from his account, but it can't be from him. It can't."

Concern lined Max's eyes and mouth. "Isn't he—" He cleared his throat. "I mean, Char said . . ."

I nodded. "He's dead."

Ella pulled the sleds around the floor, the plastic scraping over hardwood. Maybe I should tell her to stop. Maybe it would make scratches in the expensive finish. But somehow, I didn't think Max cared.

"Can we go sledding now, please?" she begged.

"Soon," Max assured her, not turning from me. "But first, I got you some Fruit Loops. They're in the kitchen. I already opened the box. Go ahead and have some."

"Yay, sugar cereal!" She dashed away, probably afraid I'd try to stop her if she didn't grab it fast enough.

Max lowered himself into a nearby chair. "What did the email say?"

I turned my phone to show him the brief message: *Where are you?*

I watched him read it, then said, "I know it's not much." But it was enough. Enough to set me on edge. Ruin my day. "What bothers me is that it came from his account."

"When was it sent? Maybe he sent it before he—"

"No, it was sent this morning."

Max nodded. "Could he have scheduled it to go out?"

"Why would he? That makes no sense." I clenched my hand. "Someone's trying to upset me."

From his grim expression, Max appeared to agree. "Who do you think sent it?"

"Someone who could easily get—or already had—access to his account. Which means it's probably someone in his family. I'm guessing his brother. I could see him doing something like this." I gave a short, dry laugh. "Not that that makes me feel much better."

"He and his family don't know where you're at?" Max paused. "You haven't been in contact with them at all?"

I shook my head.

"Why not?"

"They think I killed Connor." My voice rasped. "They hate me. They don't trust me with my own daughter. They'd take her if they could, and I don't trust them." They'd always looked the other way when Connor treated me poorly. Made excuses.

I shook my head. "I'm not going to reply to it, obviously, so I don't know what they think they're accomplishing. Besides stressing me out." Sighing, I tucked the phone in my pocket. "I'm sorry. I'm over-reacting."

"No. You have a right to be upset. Try not to let them get to you. I know it's easier said than done, but believe me, if I wasted headspace on every odd message I got, I'd have no space left in my brain. Big as it is," he added with a grin.

I managed a slight smile to show I appreciated his attempt at humor.

"And if you think about it—if that's all they've got to try to get to you—they've got nothing."

I nodded and pulled in a breath. "Thanks." I gripped the chair arm, ready to stand. "Now I'd better stop Ella before she inhales a week's worth of sugar and food coloring." My gaze darted back to him. "Thanks again for letting us stay here."

"You bet. No worries. Stay as long as you need." He touched my arm. The gentle gesture felt so nice that I struggled not to read into it.

"And hey," he added, "I also want you to know I'm sorry about your husband. About what happened. That you lost him."

"Thanks." I bit my lip, unsure how to word what I wanted him to know. "But we lost each other long ago. Our relationship, our marriage . . . it was already dead. The night he died . . . I was leaving him."

Max's brow creased and his lips thinned. With disapproval? Judgment?

I'd probably said too much. But harsh as the truth was, I felt freer for admitting it.

Ella reappeared with her cheeks bulging like a chipmunk's. "Cam we go slebbin' mow?"

Before I could correct her for talking with her mouth full, Max met my eyes. "What do you say? Should we hit the hill? I've gotta admit, I'm excited to see if we can catch some air."

Ridiculous as the thought was, it broke my somber

mood. I lifted an eyebrow. "And what about my supposed concussion?"

"Right." He looked conflicted. "Well, you should take it slow. Or just watch. But we"—he turned to Ella and held out his hand for a high five—"we're gonna fly, right?"

"Right!" She slapped his palm and beamed. Bright cereal colors dotted her teeth.

The crisp outside air was just the change I needed. I hung back near a brick firepit and watched them sailing, but when Ella begged me to join her, I couldn't resist. The rush of cold was strangely invigorating, and fresh snow provided such a soft, pillowy landing, I wasn't worried about my head. Ella yelled "Weee!" as she sat in front of me and we raced Max.

While I'd sledded with Ella in the past, and Connor had too on occasion, I couldn't remember us ever doing it together.

"Now I wanna race against you both. By myself." Ella took my sled. "You can share Max's sled."

"Come on." Max waved me over without a moment's hesitation and scooted forward, making room for me. "Little does she realize we'll go even faster with the extra weight."

I planted my hands on my hips, acting miffed. "Did you just call me extra weight?"

"What, is that offensive?" He rolled his eyes. "What I meant to say was you're so light, we'll defy gravity. We'll probably slide right back up the hill."

I flicked snow at him, but he only laughed as I settled behind him. "Yeah? Be sure to incorporate that trick into your next magic act."

He gave a short laugh, and I wished I hadn't spoken. Would he have a next magic act? Or was his career in as much danger as the internet made it seem?

"One, two, three, *go!*" Ella shot off down the hill.

We lurched forward and careened down the slope. I gripped the sides of the sled when a strange impulse made me want to grip Max. Suddenly we tilted, turned, and spilled out of the sled. I wound up on my back, winded and staring up at the gray sky, a vast expanse of clean, clear peacefulness.

Max offered his gloved hand and helped me up. I felt strangely dizzy, but in my chest, not my head. My eyes met the warmth in his, their vibrant greenness reminding me of spring.

"I won!" Ella said. So why did I feel as if I had? Where did this thrill come from? Max's fingers holding mine slightly longer than necessary?

No, the physical exertion had simply quickened my heart rate, along with the cool air rushing past. Innocent fun. That's all.

Nothing to do with this man from my past stirring up long-dormant emotions . . .

"I think I threw us off-balance," I said, blinking, still feeling all kinds of off-balance. I traipsed back up the hill and tried to focus on my steps. "Thanks for getting the sleds. That was thoughtful of you."

"Nah, purely selfish." He brushed snow from his hair. "I knew it would be fun. Sometimes a ride in the snow is all you need to clear your mind and remember what really matters."

I nodded, couldn't agree more.

"Find me!" Ella called, her voice sounding far away, and I whipped around.

She was nowhere to be seen.

My voice came out shrill and demanding. "Ella, where are you?"

"Hey." Max peered at me oddly. "It's okay. She's just playing hide-and-seek."

"I like to keep her in sight." I couldn't explain the irrational fear.

"Don't worry, she's nearby. We'll find her easily. She's probably behind those trees." He pointed, hurried over, and checked behind the trunks.

But she didn't pop out.

I rushed to a huge evergreen, its branches sweeping the ground, and peered beneath. Saw her pink boots. Relief rushed through me. "Ella."

She giggled as she crawled out.

"See?" Max strode over, and I swallowed the admonishments I wanted to release.

A simple impromptu game of hide-and-seek shouldn't set me off like this.

As we headed inside with rosy cheeks and noses, Ella said wistfully, "Hot chocolate sure would be good."

I shook my head. "She's very subtle, isn't she?"

"I like that she's not afraid to speak her mind, especially when I'm thinking the same thing." Max winked. "Hot chocolate would hit the spot. Good thing I picked some up earlier."

Inside, he started the fire and I started the hot chocolate.

The day rolled on from one comfortable distraction to the next. Max had my car towed into the driveway. That evening, I insisted on making dinner, the least I could do after all he'd done for us.

With so many groceries at my disposal, the most difficult thing about the meal was deciding what to make. I finally settled on a roast with brown gravy, mashed potatoes, and green beans with garlic butter sauce.

"Wow," Max said after tasting everything. "This is great. Where'd you learn to cook like this?"

I shrugged. "Good recipes and lots of practice." Connor expected nothing less than a home-cooked meal every night when he came home from work, so I'd had years to hone my skills. Not that I thought they were anything grand. "Anyone who can read a cookbook and follow instructions can do this."

He aimed his fork at his plate. "No, not like this, believe me. Why do you think I live on ramen and takeout?"

"You said it was because you're busy."

"Sure, too busy to waste time making recipes that end up in the trash." He took another bite. "This tastes like it came from an upscale restaurant."

Such a silly compliment to make me blush. "Thanks." I wasn't used to such appreciation and found myself rifling through recipes in my head. "So you wouldn't mind if I make more meals?"

"Mind? Are you kidding?" He put his hands on his stomach. "Even if I have to put more gym equipment in the basement to counteract the effects—totally worth it."

His words were laughable considering how trim and fit he was. I tried not to picture the muscular six-pack he likely already had.

"She makes the best cookies and cakes too," Ella added. "You should show him, Mommy. Right now."

I turned to her. "I know exactly what you're doing." I tapped her nose. "But that's enough sweets for you today."

Max finished his food, then had seconds. After dinner and dishes, we all ended up in the living room. Ella climbed onto my lap. "Read me a story, Mommy. From my fairy-tale princess book."

"Oh . . ." I stroked her hair. "I'm sorry, honey. I don't think we packed that one."

I probably should have, but I recalled passing it over in my haste to leave with only essentials.

"What?" She twisted to gape at me. "We have to go

back and get it."

The last thing I wanted was to reenter that house. I'd have to at some point, though, because I still had to arrange for it to be sold.

I twirled a wisp of her hair. "Why don't I make up a story?"

"I want my book."

"I could try telling you a story," Max offered, surprising me. But then, he did like to entertain.

Perking up, Ella faced him. "Can it be about a princess and a magician?"

He rubbed his jaw. "I could probably manage that, if you promise to help me with the princess part."

"Okay." She snuggled close to my chest. "And put a dragon in it too, because it's better with some scary stuff."

"Got it. One fire-breathing dragon." His eyes twinkled. "Once upon a time . . ."

Intrigued, I settled back and couldn't help listening just as attentively as Ella.

Thirteen

"So the fierce dragon was turned into a harmless dragonfly, the princess was free to travel the world, and the magician disappeared in a puff of smoke." Waving his hands mysteriously, Max finished his story.

"And . . . she's out," I whispered.

"I don't know if I should take that as an insult or a compliment."

"A compliment, of course. The goal of a bedtime story is sleep. You just made my job a whole lot easier. But no 'happily ever after'? I'm not complaining, just curious."

"So I didn't use those words." He shrugged and propped a foot on his knee. "It's still a happy ending."

"But the princess and the magician didn't end up together."

He snorted. "So? You can't tie a magician down. And anyway, a princess is gonna want a prince."

This conversation was getting ludicrous, but I couldn't help myself. "But where did the magician go? How do we know if he's okay? Some people hate cliffhangers." I waved my finger. "Don't even think of publishing your story like that. You'll get terrible reviews."

"Ha. Good thing I have plenty of experience with negative press." He stretched his arms and put his hands behind his head, looking very comfortable. "As for what happened to the magician, he saved the kingdom and the princess. I think we can safely assume he can take care of himself."

But was he happy? Did he ever get lonely? Did he ever see the princess again? The odd thoughts rolled through my mind. I was clearly overtired. I shouldn't be hung up on make-believe questions when I had real ones to ask.

"Why'd you leave California, Max?" I leveled my gaze at him, very much wanting to hear the answer from him, not online gossip channels.

"What, can't a guy take a vacation?" Casually as he said it, a note of defensiveness still crept in.

"Is it, though?" My voice softened. "You haven't mentioned anything about going back to California."

"Why would I? I just got here."

"But don't you have a tight schedule? Shows to perform, places to be?"

"Yeah, well, I make my own schedule." He lifted his chin. "And right now, this is the only place I want to be."

The silence that followed was comfortable enough, but if I pushed on, I suspected neither the silence nor the conversation would stay that way.

But I had to know. "Did you come here to get away from something?"

He tilted his head and eyed me. "What makes you ask that?"

"I read some things about you online, and they weren't exactly . . . flattering."

His brows flickered. "They often aren't."

I took a deep breath. "I guess what I really want to know is, are they true?"

"All depends what you read."

I wet my lips. "There were quite a few headlines about your wild drinking and terrible temper."

"Of course there were. Someone's gotta make sure the world doesn't forget I've made mistakes."

My stomach sank. "So it's true?"

"That I've made mistakes? Sure."

"No, I mean . . . the drinking and anger issues."

He studied me a long moment. "You might have Charlene beat for sounding the most disappointed."

"I . . . I just—" My shoulders went limp. "I'm surprised."

"But mostly disappointed." He paused and glanced away. "I try not to drink, but I won't lie and say I never have, that it's never gotten the best of me or brought out my temper."

"Is that what happened recently? Is that why your assistant left?"

"It's complicated."

"Okay." I waited for more. "Could you tell me about it?"

His smooth expression gave no clue as to his thoughts. He nodded at Ella sleeping in my arms. "Don't you need to get her to bed?"

"She's fine." I kept my eyes on him. "I'd really like to know what happened."

"Why? To see if I'm safe to be around? Because if that's what this is about, I can return your rent. I don't want you feeling like you have to stay if you don't want to."

But I did want to. That was the problem. I wanted to be able to justify it. "For this arrangement to work, we should be able to discuss things. Can't you tell me what happened? I won't tell anyone, if that's what—"

"I don't want to talk about it." The words came out clipped. Harsh.

Recoiling slightly, I willed my body not to overreact, not to panic. A slight indication of temper did not mean he was about to lose it.

I dropped my gaze to Ella, glad sleep had kept her insulated from his rough tone. I gripped my phone, about to leave, when paranoia made me check my email one more time, as I had periodically throughout the day—though not nearly as much as I would have without all the distractions.

Spotting a new message, I pulled in a sharp breath.

Max dropped his foot to the floor and leaned forward. "What?"

It took me a moment to find my voice. "I got another

one. Another email from Connor's account."

Swallowing, I turned the screen Max's way. He crossed the floor to see. At the same time, I reread the words in my mind:

I'll find you.

"Lame intimidation tactics," Max muttered, frowning. "Block the email address."

I hovered over the option. "I could, but that won't stop them from thinking they're getting through, and wouldn't it be better for me to know?"

"It's not worth the stress it's causing you."

I blew out a breath. Was I overreacting? "It's not like it's a threat." It just felt that way.

Who wanted to find me?

And what if they did?

I shivered, drew Ella closer, and glanced around at the wide, curtainless windows. Though I knew the vast wilderness and frozen lake stretched to the distant shore, I saw us reflected in the slick black pane, illuminated by the room's light. If someone was out there, they'd be able to see in. "What kind of security does this place have?" I didn't recall seeing any kind of system.

"Locks. And me."

I didn't say it, but I expected more from a famous person. But then, maybe Max had never felt threatened the way I did.

He stood beside me. "Hey, don't let this get to you. That's what he wants."

"Or she." I thought of Shelly. The woman I tried so hard not to think about. I didn't need more emotional turmoil. I was the one who'd been betrayed and hurt, but she didn't see it that way. Could this message be some kind of twisted retaliation against me, the woman she despised? "All I know for sure is it can't be Connor."

I glanced down at Ella, my gaze tracing her ear, the unique shape reminding me of Connor's. She slept silently. That's how I'd last seen him. Sleeping, not dead. A chill ran down my spine.

Max nodded. Rubbed his chin. Appeared about to speak, then paused. "Sorry for asking this, but did you ever actually see the body? Identify him?"

My blood drained. "His family did that. I was never asked to." Not that I would've wanted to. I'd been glad to be spared that as well as the gruesome murder scene. Imagining it was bad enough. I squeezed my eyes shut against the image. "There's a death certificate. The police are investigating his murder. I was at the funeral, saw him buried." My eyes snapped back open. "You can't mean you think it's possible he's still alive."

"I'm not saying it's not a far-fetched theory. But stranger things have happened. It's always smart to consider all angles. See through any possible smoke and mirrors."

I stared at him, hating this horrible idea. I'd gone from feeling bad to incredibly worse. "Gosh, thanks. I'm going to sleep so peacefully tonight."

He squeezed my shoulder. "Hey, I'm sorry. It's just a crazy thought, probably nothing to it. It would take an incredibly elaborate plot to pull something like that off, and for what? I'm sure the message is just from a relative, like you said."

Silence surrounded us, except for the crackling fire.

"Either way, this is a good place to lay low. Figure things out." He lowered himself to my level and met my gaze with an honesty that made him appear almost vulnerable. "That's what I'm doing here—to answer your earlier question. And I'm sorry I was short with you. I'll tell you what happened back in California if you still want to know."

I nodded, appreciating his willingness to turn my mind from my troubles by talking about his.

He pulled a wingback chair close, destroying the room's perfectly designed layout, and sank into it. "So... my assistant. Leslie."

He scanned the room as if searching for the right words. "The public loves her. Always has. My act's popularity doubled since she joined four years ago. We worked well together and things were going great, un- til"—his mouth tugged ruefully to one side—"they weren't."

Apprehension slid through me. "What happened?"

"She wanted more than a professional relationship. I didn't." Max ran his knuckles back and forth across the arm of his chair. "I guess we should've ended things right then, but I didn't think it was a big deal. She didn't act like it was."

I nodded at his baffled expression, though I wasn't perplexed. She'd likely wanted to save face by downplaying the situation, shielding her pride and her heart.

"The other night when we were discussing the magic act over dinner, she talked me into some drinks. Too many." He paused, and his head dipped so I couldn't see his face. "Next thing I knew, she was coming on to me. When I shut her down, she got angry, spiteful. Said how could I not want her when every other guy did? What's wrong with me?"

His jaw tightened and he lifted his head. His eyes darkened. "She brought up Char. Like she was jealous of her. The stuff she said was so outrageous—"

He gave an almost violent shake of his head as if to rid himself of the memory. "I lost it. We were in a private room, but still, everyone in the restaurant heard me. I didn't touch her, but I saw red. Flipped the table. Scared her and half the place. She tore out of there like I was a monster."

Picturing the scene, I tried not to cringe.

"The media had a field day." Max dragged a hand through his hair. "Trashed my reputation. Not that I don't deserve it." His lips pressed into a grim line. "They say any publicity is good, but not this time. I don't think the public will ever want me back. Especially not without Leslie."

I swallowed hard and said what I didn't want to. "Have you tried talking to her, working things out?"

"She won't talk to me. Not only that, she took out a restraining order. To top everything off, my best secrets are being leaked. I'm sure it's her, but I don't have proof." He spread his hands. "And it's not so much the secrets—plenty of people know or suspect the solutions behind the tricks. It's her betrayal that really gets me."

Oh, I knew the feeling all too well.

"For me to make a comeback, I'm going to need to come up with something phenomenal. And that still might not be enough."

He exhaled loudly. "Anyway, there you have it. I messed up. And now I'm in exile." He huffed a small laugh. "While my poor manager scrambles with damage control."

Exile? Was that how he saw it? "I'm sorry." A desire to comfort him filled me. If I wasn't still holding Ella, I'd lay a reassuring hand on his arm and tell him it would be okay.

He met my eyes. "So now that you know the ugly truth, you gonna stick around?" He smiled sheepishly. "I promise not to flip any tables."

"Max." My voice filled with compassion. "Anyone can get angry when pushed to the breaking point. And you weren't the only one at fault."

His eyes reflected hesitant hope. "So you're not afraid of me now?"

"No. And thank you for telling me the whole story."

He shrugged a shoulder. "You kind of made me. But I'm glad you did. Felt good to tell someone."

As that sank in, I blinked. "You mean—you haven't? Not even your manager? Or Charlene? And why not everyone? They should know the truth. All the blame shouldn't be on you."

"It doesn't matter. They'd twist it. I'm not giving them more ammo, especially not anything to do with Char."

And there it was. He cared more about keeping her out of this than defending himself. That realization threaded itself through me and pulled at my heart.

I gave myself a mental shake. "But she must've heard something, and she knows you're staying here. What does she think happened?"

"Oh, she knows Leslie and I had a fight and that we split, just not the details. Same for my manager. He and Char are the only ones who know my location right now." He shifted in his seat and lowered his voice. "You still didn't tell me if you're staying."

Didn't I? The look on his face—as if it mattered to him—cemented my decision. "Well, I am. If we're going to be in exile, we might as well be in it together."

Max smiled at that, and our eyes held for a moment before Ella stirred in my arms. Dropping my gaze, I maneuvered to lift her. "I'd better get her to bed."

"Right." He stood and waited, ready to offer assistance carrying her. Petite as she was, I didn't need any help. But it sure was nice knowing he was there if I did.

Fourteen

"You'll have lots of fun, you'll see. I can't wait to hear all about it when I pick you up." I leaned down and kissed Ella's cheek, struggling to hide my own hesitation.

It had taken me days of wading through a swamp of doubt to finally enroll Ella in school. Now a few days in, and I believed I was still more nervous than she was.

No matter how much I wanted to keep her glued to my side, I knew she needed interaction with other kids. Despite the hours I'd spent occupying her with all sorts of activities, she was still restless.

This would be good for her.

The kindergarten teacher smiled and led her to a large desk where two other kids sat coloring.

Returning to my car without Ella beside me still felt wrong. I glanced back, reassured by the locks and intercom system. No unidentified visitors would be admitted. She'd be fine.

I'd talked to Detective Bale, and she'd assured me Connor's body had been identified by multiple family members. Which didn't entirely comfort me, because what if they were in on some kind of cover-up? But with nothing but wild doubts, I didn't share them with her. I wasn't eager to come across as a conspiracy theorist.

The police still didn't know who'd killed Connor or why, though they seemed to be favoring the robbery-gone-wrong angle.

As Max had suggested, I'd blocked all emails from Connor's account. I'd received no more, and my worry was gradually subsiding.

I started my car and headed for the heart of the little town. Snow dusted the ornate lamp posts, benches, and store awnings, and a sign announcing an approaching ice festival made me smile. Probably the best thing a Wisconsin town could offer in January. Despite the cold, a few people strolled the sidewalks. One man walked a golden retriever wearing a bright sweater. Chilly as the scene was, its peacefulness warmed me.

I spotted Early Riser Bakery, and it called to me. A charming illustration of a loaf of bread topped with a curl of steam adorned its sign.

The smells alone were worth the stop, and I had to limit myself to purchasing a bag of rolls, because I wanted to buy everything. I asked if they were hiring, then filled out an application, something I'd been doing at various businesses in town over the last couple of days.

Once I had a job lined up, I'd find my own place and start looking into nursing programs. My life was finally starting to come together, a wonderful but surreal feeling. Like if I blinked wrong, it might all disappear.

But no, I had control of my life now. With focus, hard work, and prayer, I could reach my goals. Smiling, I headed for the grocery store to pick up what I needed for tonight's meal.

I truly enjoyed cooking when someone wasn't demanding I do it. Max was so appreciative, always insisting on taking care of the cleanup. And he even got Ella to help willingly. Which probably had something to do with how much time they spent hanging spoons on their noses.

But I wasn't complaining.

Back on the road after shopping, I noticed the vehicle behind me looked slightly familiar, but I wasn't sure when I'd first seen it. When leaving the school? The bakery? I increased my speed, then relaxed as the car faded from view.

But two intersections later, it was back. I swallowed and slowed, but the car didn't pass.

I made a sudden turn into a bank parking lot. The vehicle didn't follow. I tried to catch a glimpse of the driver as he or she drove past but couldn't from my vantage point.

With my shoulders tensing, I wound through the little town and didn't head back for the lake house till I was certain no one was following.

"What's up? You look stressed," Max said when I entered the kitchen.

"Just a little concerned." I set down my purse and four

shopping bags. "I thought I was being followed."

He crossed to my side as I told him about the car.

"Did you get the license?"

"No, the driver was always behind me. I didn't have a chance."

Max started unpacking the bags. "I wouldn't worry. It was probably nothing." He put away some cans and boxes of pasta, then grabbed an apple from the fridge and bit into it.

I wished I could put my unease away as simply as tucking packages into the pantry. I noticed papers spread all across the dining table. "What've you been up to?"

"Oh, going over ideas. Possibilities for revamping my show. Searching for a new spin on an old classic." He tossed the apple high, then caught it behind his back. "No luck yet."

I approached the table and spotted some words amid the messy sketches and scrawl.

Buried alive. Bullet catch.

A new worry took hold of me. "You wouldn't put yourself in danger just for a trick, would you?"

Max shrugged and dumped his apple core in the garbage. "The best tricks all have some element of danger."

"They do?"

"Sure. That's what draws in the crowds."

"So do funerals." I shook my head. "No career is worth dying for."

"Relax. You don't know how much risk is really involved."

"Okay." I leveled my gaze at him. "So how much is? Two percent? Twenty? Fifty? And how much is too much?"

He smiled without looking amused. "If I ever decide, I'll let you know." He swept the papers into a pile and tapped them into a neat stack. "I'm gonna head downstairs to work. Let me know if you need anything."

I huffed a breath out my nose. If he didn't care about his safety, why should I?

But I did.

I wanted to follow and lecture him, but when did that ever convince anyone? I brooded as I finished putting away groceries and made a flatbread pizza for lunch. It was more than enough for me, so I texted Max and let him know he was welcome to the leftovers.

By the time he appeared, I had something else on my mind. "Do you keep guns in the house?"

He loaded pizza slices onto a plate. "Why do you ask?"

"There's a child staying here." It hadn't occurred to me to ask until I'd mulled over the bullet-catch trick. "Please tell me that if you do, you keep them locked up."

He scowled. "Of course. I'm not stupid."

"Attempting to catch a bullet doesn't exactly sound smart."

"And we're back to that." He tossed an olive in his mouth. "I can assure you, I take every safety precaution.

And I would never put you or Ella at risk in any way. Thanks for lunch." He took his plate of food and returned to the basement.

I shook my head, beyond disappointed. Our friendship had been going so well until now.

After cleaning the kitchen, I called Charlene. We chatted a little, then I asked, "Do you know how dangerous the tricks are that Max does? Some of the ones he's considering sound awful."

She sighed. "I try not to think too much about it. He's always been attracted to risk, and trying to talk him out of anything rarely works. I pray for him, especially with what happened recently. I'm afraid he thinks he needs to prove himself to the world. I feel better knowing you're there, though. I think it helps keep him a little more grounded."

"I don't know about that." I walked to the windows and stared at the snowy deck. "I was hoping you'd talk some sense into him. He's thinking of doing a bullet-catch trick or being buried alive."

Silence lingered before she spoke. "People have died attempting those tricks. I once tried to get him to promise he'd never try them. Thanks for telling me. I'll talk to him."

I hung up feeling a little better. If anyone could convince him, she could.

* * *

I'd just walked in the door with Ella after school when Max rounded the corner and leaned against the wall. "I don't appreciate you running to my sister. I don't need people throwing roadblocks in my creative process."

"I just thought it was important that you don't take unnecessary risks. You don't have to prove yourself to anyone."

He straightened. "Actually, I do if I'm going to have any chance of saving my career."

"But it's not worth it if you"—I hesitated—"lose yourself in the process."

He opened his mouth, but Ella spoke before he could. "Mommy, look what I got!" Oblivious to the tension between us, she held up a bent envelope with her name on it. "Can I open it?"

"Sure." I tried to focus on that instead of Max. Like at her previous school, birthday invitations were periodically sent home in backpacks. This would be just the thing to help her make new friends.

But instead of a pretty card, she pulled out a sheet of folded white paper. She opened it and tried to sound out the words, which I read in an instant.

I snatched the paper away, hardly believing my eyes.

I miss you, Gabby Girl.
See you soon.
　Love,
　Daddy

Fifteen

"Give it back! It's from Daddy—I saw his name!" Ella reached for the paper.

"No." My mind spun in horrified denial. "No, sweetie." My gaze found Max's for a second before flying back to Ella. Poor, dear Ella. She didn't need this crazy, empty, confusing hope. "It's a mistake. It can't be from Daddy." I gripped her arm and crouched to eye level. "Listen, this is very important. I need you to tell me how this note got in your bag."

"I found it in my sweatshirt."

What sweatshirt? I hadn't dropped her off at school with a sweatshirt. I rummaged through her bag, saw her folder, mittens, a half-eaten bag of graham crackers, and a bunched-up sweatshirt. I recognized it as hers, but . . . I'd left this one behind in our old house.

My stomach flipped. "How did this get in here?" I pulled the sweatshirt out and searched the pockets, finding nothing but traces of lint.

"What does the note say?" Ella asked.

I eyed the typed words, wishing they were handwritten and could be sent for analysis. What about fingerprints?

Was it too late now that Ella's and my hands had been all over the paper? Not like the note was a crime, but still. It felt like one.

And Gabby Girl? That was Connor's nickname for her. And Babbling Brook for me. *My too talkative girls,* he used to say, often with more irritation than kindness, leaving no doubt he meant *too*, not *two*.

But someone else could know that. His family, his friends, coworkers. Shelly. Anyone who'd ever overheard it.

"What does it say?" Ella demanded. "Tell me!"

I shook my head and stood. "It's a mistake, honey. It's not really for you."

"It is!" Ella's anger spiked my heart rate. "I know it's from Daddy. You can't keep it!" She jumped for it and my hand closed tightly, crumpling the paper.

I pulled her to me. "Daddy's gone, remember?"

She struggled and pounded my side. "No! You just say that 'cause you want him to be! You didn't like him."

I gasped. Where was this coming from? In the two weeks since he'd died, she'd never lashed out like this.

Perhaps it was time. Perhaps the loss was finally sinking in.

"Daddy isn't coming back," I said gently, struggling to remain composed. "He's dead. We said goodbye at the cemetery."

"I want to see him!" she screamed, red-faced.

Grief engulfed me. What had happened to my sweet,

even-tempered girl?

I tried to comfort her, but she fought me. My blood roared through my head. I couldn't hear, couldn't think. "Enough, Ella. You need to calm down."

"No!"

The time for reasoning was over. I swept her into my arms, alarmed by the force of her flailing limbs, and hurried into the bedroom, where I released her on the bed.

"You need to calm down."

She cried wildly and beat the mattress with her fists.

I left, closing the door behind me, only slightly muffling her tantrum. I rubbed my forehead and pulled in a few deep breaths.

"You okay?"

I'd forgotten about Max. He still stood near the kitchen, a frown on his face but no judgment. Thankfully. I couldn't have taken that.

"This isn't like her. I'm sorry."

"Hey, she's a kid. She gets to lose it every now and then. Especially with what she's been going through. Don't worry, I don't think she'll kick any holes in the wall like I did at that age."

I wasn't so sure, but I pressed the wadded paper onto the counter and pulled out my phone, my anger turning to the school. Struggling to control my tone, I explained to the secretary that a disturbing note had made its way home with my daughter, and I wanted to know how.

The woman spoke slowly, as if still absorbing the information. "We don't know anything about a note, but her father did drop off her sweatshirt."

"Her *father*?" My mouth slackened. "Her father is dead."

The woman gasped.

"Didn't you ask for ID?"

She paused. "No, he didn't ask to come inside, you see. Just buzzed and set the sweatshirt on the cart in the vestibule, said his daughter forgot it, so he was dropping it off. I said I'd make sure she got it. I gave it to her teacher."

She rushed on, as if sensing my disapproval. "I only spoke to him for a moment, didn't think anything of it. Children leave things at home all the time—boots, lunches, homework—and parents drop them off."

Without so much as a security check?

No use berating her. It was done. Maybe she could still help. "Did you get a good look at him? Could you identify him from a photo?"

"No, I'm sorry. He was across the room, on the other side of the glass. I think he wore a hat and sunglasses, and his head was down."

And she didn't think that was suspicious? To be fair, she probably saw countless people each day. She wouldn't read into such benign details.

"There must be security footage, though, right? Could I look at that?"

A pause. "This is all very unsettling. Was the note threatening? Should we report it to the police?"

She brought the principal into the discussion, and then the police, who said I could bring in the note, file a report, and view the school footage.

It made me feel a little better. And by the time I was off the phone, Ella was quiet.

"I'll go with you to the station." Max pushed off from the wall, not even pretending he hadn't heard everything. "We can get dinner after. You deserve a meal you don't have to make."

The incident had already exhausted me, making it doubtful I'd be able to focus on anything else tonight. "Okay. I'll check on Ella and get ready."

She lay on the bed, the blanket askew. I sat beside her and set my hand on her shoulder. "Ella? Are you awake?"

She wiggled her head and grunted, and I rubbed her back soothingly. After a few moments, she turned her head to me, her eyes red. "I miss Daddy." She wiped her nose on the blanket. "I don't want him to be gone."

"Oh, honey." I leaned down and drew her into my arms. "I know, and I'm sorry."

She sniffed and tears fell. My heart ached for her. For us. The family we could've been.

"Why did someone hurt him, Mommy? Why? I want to know."

"I don't know, honey. Even if we knew, it wouldn't change the fact that he's gone."

He *is* gone, I told myself.

Wishing I could give Ella some closure, I stroked her hair back from her face and dried her tears with my thumbs.

"Would you like to visit Daddy's grave and bring him some flowers? We could say some prayers and you could tell him how much you miss him." It was out before I could think it through. The last thing I wanted was to go back to that town, revisit that pain.

But if it would help bring Ella comfort, closure, and healing, I would do it. As many times as she needed.

Sixteen

Ella remained subdued at the police station, as if her blowup had taken too much out of her. Or maybe the solemn atmosphere of the place intimidated her. I was grateful for Max, who distracted her in the waiting area with a Rubik's Cube.

The school's security footage was useless—a low-quality recording of a man in jeans and a dark coat, hat, and sunglasses. Nothing unique to distinguish him by. With no audio, I couldn't even attempt to recognize a voice.

I was glad to leave, but I didn't feel like I'd accomplished anything.

Max parked near FlapJack's Diner, then led the way inside. Vinyl records decorated the walls along with framed photographs of singers and actors. Retro music played from the speakers above.

Max sat with his back to the room, and I found myself wondering if it was a conscious choice.

"Are you worried someone will recognize you?" I asked as Ella and I slid into the booth.

"Not worried, but I'd prefer they don't."

I glanced at an old man in a denim shirt eating at the counter. A middle-aged couple sat across from each other near the back of the room. The only curious eyes were mine.

Max followed my gaze. "Seems like a quiet place. People keep to themselves. Which is one of the reasons I chose this town." He smiled. "That and the awesome name. Plus they have a magic shop. Not many towns do."

A young waiter with a prominent Adam's apple took our order and gave us tall glasses of ice water complete with lemon wedges. When the food arrived, Ella poked glumly at her macaroni, which she usually loved.

Max took the saucer from an unused coffee mug and squeezed his lemon into it.

I paused with a crusty bread slice at my lips. "What are you doing?"

"You'll see." He twisted his clean paper napkin into a stubby stick, then dipped the end in the lemon juice and proceeded to write with it on the back of his paper placemat. "Some people make lemonade out of lemons. I prefer to make invisible ink."

"Invisible?" Ella perked up. "Like, no one can see it?"

"That's right." He lowered his voice and leaned forward. "Which means it's perfect for writing secret messages. You have to know the special trick to make the writing appear."

Ella's eyes rounded. "What is it?"

"Once the writing dries, I'll show you. It should be

ready by the time we finish eating."

Ella nibbled several bites. "Is it ready yet?"

"Soon."

She bounced impatiently in her seat but managed a few more bites. "Now?"

"Almost."

After another few forkfuls, Max gave a thumbs-up. "All we need is a heat source." He lifted the paper to the low-hanging lamp above our table. Not exactly the best way not to call attention to himself.

"A light bulb is perfect, but be careful not to touch it and burn yourself. Only do this with a grown-up's help."

Slowly, faint tan letters appeared and darkened to a golden brown.

Ella grinned. "Cool! Can I read it?"

"Go ahead and try." Max handed it to her. "I'm not known for neat handwriting."

"'Who,'" Ella read, brow scrunched, "'wants . . . dessert?'"

I laughed, as much at the trick as at Ella's expression.

"Me!" she said. "And can I try writing something? Does it work for pictures too?"

"You bet. And if you don't have lemons, milk works just as well."

I could just imagine how much fun she was going to have with her next glass of milk. There'd be more on the paper than in her, but I mouthed "Thank you" to Max and meant it. Not just for dessert—tall milkshakes with huge swirls of whipped cream topped with sprinkles and shiny cherries—but for the distraction that had brightened my little girl's face.

He really did have a magic touch.

Back at the house, after her bath, Ella asked for her fairy-tale princess book again, and I compromised by letting her watch a show. She chose *Frosty the Snowman*.

She tugged Max's hand. "Will you watch it with us? There's a magician in it."

"Yeah? How could I say no to that?"

And so we all ended up on the couch munching popcorn, Ella between us, as the animated classic captured her attention.

A few minutes in, she climbed onto my lap, leaving little space between me and Max. I tried not to focus on his nearness, how cozy this was.

"See, he has a magic hat and a rabbit." Ella pointed to the bumbling cartoon magician, a most unflattering character with a laughably large nose and chin. "I still want to see you do that trick."

"I don't know." Max scratched his head, then spoke to me out of the corner of his mouth. "This has me seriously rethinking my career choice." He nudged me a few moments later. "Should I grow a mustache like that?" His eyebrows bounced in amusement as he pretended to twirl an evil-villain mustache, and I held in a laugh.

"I'm glad you're not a meanie like that magician," Ella announced at the end.

"Not as glad as I am." Max gave an exaggerated grimace.

"If I build a snowman, could you bring it to life?"

"If I ever figure out how, you'll be the first to know."

"Come on," I said, easing Ella to the ground, though reluctant to move myself. "Enough stalling. It's time for bed."

After helping her get settled, I returned to the living room to clean up the stray popcorn. Max stood staring out the large window, as if he could see the lake through the darkness.

I suddenly felt a need to break the silence. "Sorry if you have the Frosty song stuck in your head all night. I know I will."

He didn't answer, and I moved to his side. "What are you looking at?" All I saw was our reflection in the glass, as if our images were trapped in a slab of black ice.

"Nothing."

"You seem rather fixated for nothing."

"Just thinking. And I thought I saw a light in the neighbor's cottage. Never seen that before."

I squinted. "I don't see anything. Do you know who lives there?"

"No, never met them. I think it's just another vacation place, not occupied year-round."

I slid my gaze from our reflection. "Thanks for cheering Ella up today."

"She's quite a kid."

"Thank you. This has been hard on her."

"And you." He turned and touched my arm. "She's lucky to have you. Whoever's been trying to scare you . . . remember, it's just that. An attempt. Don't let them get to you."

I nodded, then moistened my lips. "I promised Ella I'd take her to visit Connor's grave tomorrow."

Silence followed, and I wondered what Max was thinking.

His eyes tightened with concern, like he knew how much I dreaded the trip. "Do you want me to come?"

Yes.

But I shouldn't. The fact that the desire popped so strongly into my heart told me I had no business entertaining it. This spark of attraction—I couldn't deny it. But I could deny it the opportunity to grow. Had to.

The very thought of visiting my husband's grave with another man was enough to make me imagine Connor haunting me. Not that I believed in such things. In fact, I wasn't even one hundred percent sure he was dead. And that thought chilled me the most.

I stepped back. "No. Thanks for the offer, but we need to do this alone."

Max nodded.

"I'd better get some sleep. Good night." I retreated to my room and tried my best to shut my brain down for the night.

I'd gladly take the Frosty song on repeat over these

unsettling thoughts.

In bed, my disturbed mind morphed memories into unwelcome dreams.

If you ever leave me, I'll find you. Connor's eyes flashed. *I'll kill you.* He drew back and slammed his knuckles into the wall. Inches from my face. Noise exploded in my ears.

I choked on a scream and flinched awake, certain I'd narrowly missed his fist for real. My gaze darted, searching the shadows.

Ella's hand seized my arm. "Mommy, what was that?"

My heart raced. "Nothing, I just had a bad dream. Sorry for waking you."

"But I heard something. A loud bang."

Fear curled my stomach. So I hadn't dreamed the noise?

I strained to hear above my pounding heart. "It's okay," I whispered, not believing myself. My hand darted to the light switch and felt a small measure of comfort when illumination bathed the room and revealed nothing.

No intruder.

No Connor.

Still, I slid my phone from the nightstand, ready to dial for help.

I threw open the closet, checked the bathroom, peered under the bed, and cracked the window shade. Saw only the black pane. I'd have to turn off our light to look out properly, and I didn't want to. My skin crawled and I let the slats fall shut.

I tried calling Max's phone, but he didn't answer. I debated what to do, pondered what I'd really heard. A loud bang of some kind. Against the door, the wall, or possibly the window. Inside or out? Either way, I wasn't about to leave Ella alone and investigate.

She stared at me. "What was it?"

"Probably a tree branch. I think it's windy tonight." Was it? Why didn't we hear anything now?

I double-checked our bedroom lock, dimmed the light, and sat beside Ella, still holding my phone like a lifeline. I stroked her back, the steady motion gradually soothing us both. At least she could go back to sleep.

The next morning, a knock on the bedroom door jolted me awake.

"Brook, Ella? You okay in there?"

More sleep was all I wanted. It took me a long moment to orient myself to my surroundings. Forcing my eyes open, I saw Ella stirring.

A measure of relief descended. We'd made it safely through the night. A touch of embarrassment followed. "We're fine."

Max's voice came through the door. "Usually I'm the late sleeper, but I saw you tried calling me at one in the morning."

I set my feet on the cold floor. "A loud bang woke us up. I wondered if you heard it and if we should check it out." I finger-combed my hair hastily, threw on my clothes, and opened the door.

"Sorry, I sleep through almost anything." Max looked regretful, his disheveled hair and pajamas making me think he'd rushed to check on us the second he saw my call.

Something about that both comforted and concerned me.

"I guess it was nothing anyway." I crossed the room and pulled up the shade.

Only to stifle a screech.

Smeared on the window in what looked like blood, ugly dark letters spelled an unmistakable message:

Found you.

Seventeen

Anger and fear trembled through my limbs even after the police left.

I tried for Ella's sake to act like it was nothing. But she knew better. The last few weeks had taught her that when bad things happen, cops appear.

Max and I had tried to keep her shielded from the discussion, but she clutched my hand and didn't want to leave my side.

The police examined the window, tested the substance, and didn't seem surprised by the results.

"Sure enough, fake blood," an officer said. "Easy to make or buy." He regarded me briefly. "You know anyone who might want to scare you like this?"

Names ran through my head, and I shared my concern that the incident was connected in some way to Connor's case, to his family or friends. The officer listened patiently but didn't say much more than that the department would look into it. Which didn't give me the comfort I needed.

Because on the list of priorities for a small police department, I knew this little incident lay near the bottom.

Yet the message, though wiped away, remained in my mind, unnerving me.

Who had found me?

Connor?

No, not possible.

Another hand took mine—too big to belong to Ella—and I blinked the worried haze from my mind to meet Max's concerned gaze.

"Hey. How're you doing?"

I swallowed. "I thought we'd be safe here. That no one would know where we were . . . That we could start over."

"You are safe. I promise." The strength of his words told me he meant it.

"But you can't promise that. No one can. Not even the police." Through the front door, I watched the last of them drive away. "Not when we don't know who's doing this or why."

He squeezed my hand. "Someone's just trying to spook you."

"And what if they decide to step it up and do something worse?"

His jawline hardened. "I won't let that happen."

"But that's not in your control. Whoever this is, they found Ella at school. They found us here. I don't feel safe anywhere." I removed my hand, not because I wanted to, but because I didn't.

"Maybe we should leave." As I said them, the words carved a pit in my stomach. "Maybe we should go back to Bloomington. This person knows where we are any-way, so what's the difference?"

"The difference is I'm here. You shouldn't be on your own right now."

"I shouldn't be pulling you into this."

"You're not—they are. If I can help you and Ella, that's all I care about."

His words made me pause. He cared about us. He really did. And while that touched me in a way I could hardly comprehend, I needed to be the one protecting my daughter. I shouldn't be relying on him. No matter how tempting.

"Mommy, can we still visit Daddy today?"

I pulled in a breath. I'd promised. And distraction was better than stewing. "Sure, sweetie. Let's eat and get ready."

While Ella brushed her teeth, I paced beside Max. "I have to find out who's been sending these messages and why. If it is Connor's family, it's time I let them know I won't put up with it."

Max pulled on his coat. "I'm coming with you."

I didn't argue.

Just outside of Bloomington, we stopped at a grocery store to pick up a bouquet of flowers for the grave. Ella chose a gaudy bunch of artificially colored gerbera daisies. "I want Daddy to see them all the way from heaven," she said matter-of-factly.

At the cemetery, I drove past the slanting and broken

headstones of the older plots. Gravelly snow crunched under our tires. The wind tried to blow the door closed on me when I stepped out, and Max hurried to hold it. No one had done such a gentlemanly thing for me since . . . when?

Too long.

Ella hugged her flowers protectively and marched to the fresh grave with a determination that made me both proud and sad. My little girl, forced to grow up and face stark realities sooner than she should.

I shivered and Max moved closer, partially blocking the cold. Snowflakes whirled low to the ground on wisps of wind, like gauzy, fluttering ribbons. I stared down at the bleak grave. How was it that someone as tall and imposing as Connor could leave so little impression? Just a small, blank plot in this stretch of stone-studded land. He didn't even have a headstone yet.

And if I died today, what would I leave? My dear Ella, without any parents. I had to fight my fears so I could be the best mother for her, a wall against the cruelties of the world. And more than that, someone to guide her with love to true peace and happiness.

I bowed my head and clasped her shoulders, lifting my heart to God, asking for mercy and protection for her. Sun filtered from the clouds, rays of warmth through the frigid day. And almost like a whisper came the thought that I shouldn't forget to pray for myself.

Ella set the flowers down and brushed away snow to

reveal assorted items left by others who'd visited the grave.

Blue silk roses. A beer-fest mug. A hockey puck from Connor's favorite team. And a heart-shaped faux stone engraved with the word *Son*.

For all his flaws, he was loved and missed.

Ella gazed around as if looking for something. In a small voice, she said, "I thought maybe I'd see Grandma and Grandpa here."

That hit me hard. She was missing them because of me. "Would you like to see them today, Ella?"

"Really?" She looked up to see if I was serious.

Maybe I'd been wrong to keep her from them. She loved them. And despite their shortcomings, I didn't doubt they loved her.

"Really." Perhaps we could put an end to all this unpleasantness. Perhaps it could be as simple as a conversation. I had to try. Maybe the time that had passed was enough for their tempers to settle and reason to set in.

About fifteen minutes later, we pulled up to their place, a small blue ranch home trimmed with assorted colored stones. Near the garage stood an old basketball hoop, the backboard faded to gray and the worn net hanging askew.

We walked up steep steps to the porch, past an old-fashioned statue of a boy holding a lantern.

Standing tall and firm, my hand on Ella's shoulder, I

pressed the doorbell and willed my heartbeat to stay steady. I glanced at Max, and a tilt of his chin seemed to say, *You've got this.*

I sure hoped so.

Eighteen

Connor's mother, Barb, opened the door wearing a drab gray sweat suit. Lacking all traces of her usual makeup, she looked older. Lines around her eyes and mouth deepened and multiplied when she saw me.

But she broke into a smile for Ella. "Darling! Oh, it's so good to see you!" Barb opened her arms wide and Ella moved in for a hug.

"I thought you'd like a visit," I said. "We were in town."

"I'd like more than a visit." She hesitated with the door and I imagined she wanted to shut it on me and disappear inside with Ella, but she finally opened it farther. Not wide, but wide enough. "Come in."

"We won't stay long, but I thought it would be good for Ella to see you. I hope that's okay."

"Of course. Ella is always welcome. I wish I'd known you were coming. Ross isn't here right now." She looked at Max. "And who is this young man?"

"Name's Max." He offered his hand.

She hesitated a split second before taking it briefly. "And you are?"

"A friend." He smiled, not appearing at all disturbed by her demanding tone.

Barb released his hand and looked at me questioningly, disapprovingly. Knowing full well I'd never had any male friends when I was with Connor.

I hadn't stopped to think how this would appear. She was likely thinking the worst.

"Oh?" Barb peered down her nose at him. "What kind of friend?"

I floundered for the best answer. I could say he was a friend of a friend, but he was more than that.

"A good friend," Max answered, the corner of his mouth lifting. "No other kind worth having, right?"

I relaxed. Let her think what she wanted.

Her lips pursed, and she took Ella's hand. "Come on, darling, let's find you some cookies."

I wiped my feet and followed Barb into the kitchen, no intention of letting Ella out of my sight.

Beside the table stood Ross's art easel and a large canvas, red and black paint swirled into an abstract form that somehow left me feeling disconcerted. I guessed it was a work in progress but wasn't sure.

Ella munched molasses cookies and talked about sledding and her new friends at school. "We're going to put on a talent show."

Barb's eyes brightened. "And where is this new school? Where did you move to?"

Ella looked at me.

"Honey, why don't you go play with some of the puzzles on the rug in the living room?"

Once she was settled in sight but out of earshot, I turned to Barb. "Here's the thing." I remained standing, reminding myself to stay strong. "After everything that happened, I decided it was best to start over somewhere new. For now, I'm going to be cautious about sharing where that is. I'll bring Ella for visits as long as we can all get along."

Barb's nostrils flared. "You're creating drama where there doesn't need to be any."

I pulled in a fortifying breath. "Lately I've experienced some concerning incidents. Someone's been trying to scare me. And I just want to make sure that isn't something you or Ross or Ian would do. Do you know if they happened to go out anywhere late last night?"

"As if that's any of your business."

"I understand if you're upset, but I won't stand for threats."

"Well, that's a fine thing, coming into my home and accusing me and my loved ones." She bristled. "I won't stand for threats either."

"I'm not threatening you, just making you aware of the situation."

"If you're asking for my okay on"—she swept her gaze over Max and lowered her voice—"whatever you're doing with him, you won't get it. You should be ashamed—"

"I'm not. I don't need your okay to have a friend."

Her face reddened. "You running off right after the murder makes you look guilty. Everyone thinks so. And hiding our granddaughter from us is cruel. How can we be sure she's getting the stability, safety, and education she needs?"

"Because I'm making sure of it. I'm her mother. A good mother. And I tried to be a good wife to your son." My chest tightened. "Even when he made that difficult."

"What's that supposed to mean?"

Perhaps she didn't know. Perhaps her love for him had blinded her.

But that's not what this was about. I softened my tone. "I only want what's best for Ella."

"So do we. You may be able to move on and replace Connor like that." She snapped her fingers. "But that doesn't mean Ella should." She narrowed her eyes at Max. "What did you say your name is? Your full name?"

He returned her intense gaze with a mild one. "I didn't."

I lifted my chin. "The police told me I was free to move as long as they knew where to reach me. I want this case solved just as much as you do. But we have to go on living our lives. Ella needs that. We all do. If you want to keep seeing her, we need to get along. So I'm asking you to please talk to Ian, make sure he's not harassing me." I spread my hands. "Will you do that?"

She sniffed. "I can't make him believe something he doesn't."

"Let him know that if he is the one trying to scare me, the police are looking into it. If he's smart, he'll stop. And maybe he could give that message to Shelly too."

"Shelly?"

"He knows who she is," I said stiffly, unable to voice the ugliness. The thought of her still made my stomach flop.

I cleared my throat. "There's one more thing I need to ask . . ." And no delicate way to do it. "I'm sorry."

She compressed her lips in a way that said she doubted that.

But I was. I knew the depths of motherly love. I pulled in a breath. "Did you . . . After Connor died, did you identify his body?"

Her face turned horrified, then crumpled. "I couldn't bear it." She turned away. "Ross did, and Ian. Why would you ask such a thing?"

"I'm sorry." I touched her arm. "I really am."

"Grandma, will you read me a story?" Ella called from the other room, her timing perfect.

After the story, we said our goodbyes. Ella gave Barb a big hug and kiss, and I hoped it eased the woman's pain.

Outside, I was just getting Ella in her seat when a car pulled into the driveway.

"You know who that is?" Max asked.

I nodded, my shoulders tensing. "Ross, Connor's dad."

"Hi, Grandpa!" Ella called as he climbed out.

"Hey there, peanut." He sidled over and chatted with her for a little bit before eying me. His tone went from pleasant to accusatory. "Barb's been worried sick about her."

"I'm sorry. But we already visited with her. We were just leaving."

He grunted, and I wasn't sure how to interpret it. After telling Ella goodbye, he closed her door and aimed his angular chin at me. "You must be mighty proud of yourself, getting away with everything you did. If it weren't for that little girl . . ." His words turned to a mumble as he crossed to his car and opened the trunk.

"What was that?" Was he threatening me? I stalked after him, vaguely aware of Max following me.

Ross muttered something and reached into the trunk, past a few large sheets of curved paper, as if they'd been rolled up but had unfurled. It took me a second to realize what they were.

Targets.

Featuring human silhouettes. Riddled with bullet holes.

My eyes widened.

Maybe now wasn't a good time to confront Ross after all.

Max stepped closer, his posture nonchalant. "Nice, looks like you came from the shooting range, hey?" He put a hand on my arm and nudged me back. "What do you shoot?"

Ross pulled a black case from the trunk, then another.

"Let me guess." Max tilted his head. "A twenty-two? A thirty-eight?"

What did it matter? I searched my memory, trying to recall hearing anything about Ross owning a gun or shooting for sport.

I couldn't. My pulse quickened.

"Nope, a nine-millimeter and a forty-five." Ross rolled up the targets and tucked them under his arm, revealing a long, narrow case at the far back of the trunk.

Max nodded at it. "What about that one?"

"A rifle."

"Is it pretty accurate?"

He grabbed it. "I was hitting bull's-eyes at a thousand yards today. You tell me."

"Whoa, almost sounds like a sniper rifle."

"It is." Ross slammed the trunk and headed for the house.

"Friendly guy," Max said as we returned to my car.

Inside, I couldn't start the engine fast enough. I turned kids' songs on and drove away.

I spoke under my breath. "Is a sniper rifle something normal people shoot?"

Max seemed to choose his words carefully. "It's not unheard of."

I sensed he was trying not to worry me, like there was something he wasn't telling me. "What makes it different from other guns?"

"Well, it's for shooting from really long distances."

"So it's like what an assassin would use to take someone out without being seen?" My stomach churned. Were the Mortons that convinced I'd killed Connor? That desperate to do something about it?

"Come on, Brook. The guy probably just likes to shoot. Don't freak yourself out."

"But isn't it strange that he has it? I think it is. Is it even legal?"

"Long as he passed the background check."

"But I've never heard of him shooting before." He was just an ordinary middle-aged guy who repaired appliances, played golf, ice fished, and painted.

"So maybe he picked it up recently. Maybe he needed a new hobby."

Yeah, hunting me.

I grimaced.

Max slanted a concerned look my way. "So I'm thinking that visit didn't make you feel any better."

I adjusted my rearview mirror needlessly. "At least I said what I had to. I just hope I didn't make things worse." I glanced at Ella in the back seat. "But at least she enjoyed it."

I paused at a stop sign, then continued down the road.

Max turned slightly in his seat. "That car's been following us since we left. Now it's flashing its lights. You recognize it?"

"It's not Ross, is it?" My spine tightened as I pictured

him with his sniper sights on me.

I studied the vehicle in the mirror, then breathed a little easier. "I think it's just one of Connor's friends." Dane. But what did he want?

And did I want to know?

Nineteen

Making up my mind, I turned into a church parking lot, and Dane followed. I stopped the car with a slight jolt.

Max unbuckled and faced me. "You're sure about this?"

I nodded. After all, avoiding people hadn't worked. "He might have something important to tell me." I cracked my door to step out. "Will you stay with Ella?"

"Sure." Max sat back but didn't appear to relax. "Just give me a nod if you need me."

"But I wanna see Dane too," Ella protested.

"I have to talk to him alone, honey." I exited, closing the door before she could argue.

"Hello, Dane." I kept my voice neutral and stepped several paces from my car.

He jogged up. Wind ruffled the hair poking from the sides of his winter hat, and he ducked his head against the cold. "Brook, I thought you'd left town for good. How are you?"

"What do you want?" I crossed my arms and hugged them to my body. Any conversation in this weather needed to be brief.

Disappointment touched his face. "Don't hate me just because I'm friends with the Mortons." He paused, seemed to weigh his words. "I saw you leaving their place. Whatever you were doing over there, be careful."

As if I needed anyone telling me that after what just happened.

"You're probably right to stay away. Ian . . . he's still set on you going down for the murder. And his folks, they're serious about getting Ella. They even hired an investigator to track you down."

"An investigator?" I wanted to scoff, but I believed him. I knew I'd been followed. "Why?"

"They're trying to build a case against you. If they can get evidence of you being an unfit mother, maybe even claim you're mentally unstable, that'll help them get Ella."

Though horrified, a dry laugh popped out of me. Was that the motive behind the messages? Drive me to paranoid behavior? What legitimate PI would do such a thing?

Maybe he wasn't legit.

Then again, if he provided my whereabouts, Ian or Ross could do the rest.

"But it's worse than that." Dane lowered his voice. "They think they're going to find something to prove you're responsible for Connor's death."

Exasperation filled me. "But I wasn't even there.

There's proof."

Dane sighed, seemed to have to force out his next words. "They think you hired someone."

That left me speechless for a moment.

"I would've warned you about all this sooner, but I had no way to get in touch."

"I appreciate the heads up." I did, despite how upsetting. I crooked an eyebrow. "And they just shared all this with you because . . . ?"

"You know how close Connor and I were. I'm like one of the family. Seriously, they don't care what they say around me." He glanced behind him, gaze sweeping the parking lot and roads, then hunched his shoulders. "I overhear things. I still hang out with Ian. The family has me for dinner sometimes." His mouth dipped sadly. "I think it helps us all deal with the loss."

"So why would you betray them to help me?"

"I'm not betraying anyone, just trying to do the right thing. I'm concerned about you. Just don't let them know I told you anything." He swallowed. "Ian can be crazier than Connor."

"Crazy enough to kill his own brother and pin it on me?"

"What?" Alarm touched his voice and he drew back slightly. "You don't really think that, do you?"

"I don't know what to think. But you'd better be careful just in case."

He swallowed again. I'd already upset him. I might as

well push on. "I need to ask you something." He'd been blunt enough. I could be too. "When you and Ian found Connor that morning—you're sure it was him? And that he was—really dead?"

Dane blinked. Gave a little shake of his head as if he hadn't heard me right. "Of course. Why would you ask that?"

"I just need to be sure. I would think, after such a violent attack, it might be . . . difficult to tell."

"Of course it was *difficult*." A haunted look came over him. "Everything about it was difficult. Be glad you didn't have to see it. I have to see it every day."

He looked past me, seemed to be reining in his emotions.

"I'm sorry."

He nodded. He opened his mouth, then closed it and rubbed the back of his neck. "Maybe I shouldn't say this, but I wonder if Shelly did it. She always seemed so jealous."

I'd seen that jealousy firsthand in the few moments I'd encountered her. "I've wondered that too." I'd wondered so many things about her, each thought more painful than the last. But I couldn't process what I didn't know. Here was my chance. I pulled in a deep breath. "How did Connor meet her? How long were they . . . together?"

Dane grimaced and shifted. "You really want to know?"

"No. But I need to."

He nodded slowly. "He met her at the auto shop a few months ago. She came in for some repair work. Mid-October, I think. She kept coming back. It sounded like she was the one who pursued him, if that's any consolation."

It wasn't, not really. "Were there others?"

"No."

"You sound sure."

"I am. Connor was terrible at hiding things."

From where I stood, it seemed he'd done a pretty good job.

"From me, I mean." Dane stuffed his hands in his pockets and looked at the ground. "Just so you know, I never supported the affair. I told him so flat out. You didn't deserve that. And you shouldn't have found out the way you did."

I absorbed his words, unsure what to say. *Thank you* didn't feel appropriate.

"But he did love you, in his own way. We all have our flaws, but"—he glanced at my car—"he adored Ella." His gaze shifted, and he straightened. "Oh, I'm sorry. I didn't realize you were with someone." His gaze held a moment longer. Trying to figure out who it was?

"I won't keep you," he said. "Just, I felt I owed you—for not telling you things I should have earlier."

I did feel a measure of gratitude. He hadn't had to go out of his way to share all this. "Thanks, Dane. I'm glad I know."

He nodded. "Stay safe." He was halfway to his car when he turned back and handed me a card. "Here's my number if you need anything." He met my eyes, his full of regret. "I'll always be sorry I tried so hard to be such a loyal friend to Connor that I wasn't a good friend to you."

"That's okay. You were always kind. I understand more than most what a big and . . . assertive personality Connor had."

Dane frowned. "He didn't treat you right. I mean, not just about Shelly, but . . . I know he had a temper and could get violent. He lost it on you sometimes, didn't he? I suspected. I should've done something."

But it was easier to look the other way. I got it. I stuffed the card in my pocket, glad he didn't ask for my number, because I still didn't want to give it. "I really have to get going."

"Sure. Just—" He stepped back. "I want you to know I'm sorry. I guess that's what I really wanted to say."

"Thanks." I couldn't quite make myself smile. I turned and headed for my car. I didn't want sorrow or sympathy. I wanted strength. Courage.

"That looked intense," Max said when I returned, his gaze following Dane as he climbed into his vehicle.

I adjusted the music volume and spoke at a level only Max could hear. "Turns out I was right, I have been followed. The Mortons hired an investigator." I shared the details. "Let them waste their money. They're not going to find anything on me. Trying to prove I'm an unfit mother?" My hands clenched.

Dane waved to Ella as he drove away.

"Hi, Dane," she sang out. She'd always liked him. He used to grill burgers in the backyard with Connor while she played in the sandbox. He'd pounded on the drum set with her and Connor in the basement, dribbled basketballs with her occasionally, and even taken her fishing. "What did he want, Mommy?"

I pressed my lips together and pressed the pedal slightly too hard as I drove away. "He wanted to say hi, sweetie, and tell us . . . he misses your daddy too."

Seemingly satisfied with that explanation, Ella stared out the window for a while. "Can we visit our old house?" Her voice rose in pitch. "Can we get my fairy-tale princess book?" Her eager foot bopped my seat. "Please?"

I couldn't think of a reason to refuse, other than I didn't want to look at that house—let alone set foot in it. But I couldn't tell her that. "I'll run in and get it, but that's it. You have to promise to wait in the car."

"I can get it," Max offered, likely sensing my disdain for the place when I pulled into the driveway.

I blinked and released my seat belt. "Thanks, but I know right where to find it. It'll be easier if I do it." And faster.

Repulsion swept me the moment I opened the door. I expected more of a musty, closed-up smell. I tried to ignore the thought of where Connor's body had lain, and the blood . . .

We had walked on that floor every day for years, never knowing what was coming.

Shaking myself, I hurried up the stairs. I was certain Ella's book had been left on her bed, but I found it on the shelf.

Book in hand, I paused at the door to the master bedroom. Was it my imagination, or did I detect a whiff of Connor's cologne? How could it still be floating around?

It couldn't be.

I stepped in and my breath hitched. A drawer hung partially open. I hadn't left it like that.

"Hello?" My voice came out forcefully, compensating for the fear snaking through me. "Is someone here?"

A rustle. From the bathroom?

A shadow in the mirror.

I hurried forward just in time to catch a glimpse of someone in a striped shirt—Connor's—dash out the door and pound down the stairs.

"Stop!" I raced after the person, flew through the rooms. The back sliding door stood wide open, cold air swooshing in, flapping the drapes.

I stopped at the threshold and caught a flash of movement disappearing through trees.

Coldness engulfed me.

I couldn't catch the person, and I didn't want to.

Heart thumping wildly, I closed the door and locked it.

Twenty

It couldn't have been him. It couldn't.

Every logical part of me told me Connor was dead. But the fearful, frantic part fed off of the impossible possibility.

I hadn't even made it all the way to the car when Max stepped out, clearly reading on my face that something was wrong. As soon as I shared what I'd seen, he called the police.

"They're probably sick of hearing from me," I said now as Max drove, my mind too charged to focus on the road. The authorities had gone through the usual procedures, questioning, checking the place over. No new signs of forced entry, no signs of an intruder. They did take some pictures of footprints in the backyard, but I felt it was more to appease me than anything.

"You believe I saw someone, right?" I asked quietly.

"If you say it, I believe it. The question is, who was it? And what were they doing there?"

"Maybe it was just some random person, a squatter who realized no one's living there." Random sounded so much better than the alternative. "Maybe they wanted to rob it, and I startled them. They couldn't have known I was coming. We didn't even know. It was Ella's idea, a last-minute decision."

"I'm sorry, Mommy." Her voice came quietly from the back.

My stomach dropped. I shouldn't have forgotten she was listening. "No, honey. You have nothing to be sorry for. You didn't do anything wrong."

"But I wanted you to go there. And someone scared you. I don't care if you sell the house now. I don't want to go back."

I turned and saw her hugging her book to her chest like a security blanket.

"Maybe the person who killed Daddy lives there now."

That such a thought could even cross her mind pained me deeply. She needed reassurance so much more than I did.

I reached out and touched her leg, wishing I'd sat in the back with her. "No, sweetie, no. They couldn't. It's locked. And the police will keep an eye on it."

Not that they could spare limited resources watching an unoccupied house, and I didn't expect them to.

My arm hurt from stretching to keep a reassuring hand on Ella, but I didn't want to take away her comfort. "It was probably Uncle Ian. He probably knew how to get in with the garage code. I've changed it now, but maybe he just wanted some of your dad's things." If so, he was welcome to them.

But he wouldn't have run from me. He would've confronted me. I should count myself lucky it wasn't him.

Max crooked an eyebrow, and I could tell he was holding in what he wanted to say, for Ella's sake.

"So I've heard a lot about that book of yours," he said cheerily, "and I've gotta admit, now that you've got it, I'm kinda itching to hear one of the stories. See if they live up to the hype."

"Mommy can't read in the car. She gets carsick. It's disgusting."

"Ella!" I shot her a look, and she cracked a smile.

I glanced at Max, grateful he'd lightened the mood. Grateful for his reassuring presence. Grateful for him. Just the sight of him calmed my fears while sparking hope that things would get better.

He shouldn't be able to do all that with a mere smile. I shivered and turned away. I was becoming too attached to his presence, finding far too much comfort in it. This arrangement couldn't last. I had to remember that.

I stared out the window. "Tell me more about that talent show you mentioned, Ella."

"Lots of kids are going to sing or dance. Anita is going to do gymnastics. I want to do magic tricks. Max, will you teach me and help me practice?"

"I'd love to."

I faced him. "Don't feel pressured."

"In fact," he continued, "we can start today."

I caught an enthusiastic glimmer in his eyes and didn't want to squelch it. I set my hands on my lap. "Okay, as long as the tricks are safe. Nothing scary."

Max glanced back at Ella. "Guess that means we'll have to scrap the sawing-a-kid-in-half trick."

"Max." I whapped his arm.

"Sword swallowing?"

I shot him a look.

"Fire eating?"

"Honestly."

"The bunny-in-a-hat trick!" Ella exclaimed. "That's not scary or dangerous."

"Unless you're the bunny," I said.

"No, it's totally harmless." Max waved a hand. "Actually, bunnies love it. It's like going down a rabbit hole."

The conversation stayed on magic tricks until we stopped to eat, then picked up again when we reached Vanishing Lakes. But instead of taking the rambling road to his place, Max headed into town, slowed, and finally parked in front of a store called The Bottomless Magic Hat, which adjoined a store called The Bottomless Toy Box.

"That sounds a little scary," I said, picturing a child lured by toys and falling headlong into dark, endless nothingness.

"You kidding me? It's the best kind of store." Max hopped out and opened Ella's door. "We're going to get an awesome magic kit, right?" He held out his hand for a high five. Ella grinned and gave it.

I expected her to start clamoring for the dolls and ponies in the toy-store window, but she walked right past, following Max into the dim magic store.

A mirrored glass case held an assortment of tricks. Creepy masks lined the upper shelves. Max headed for a corner display and picked up a big windowed box containing red plastic cups, a deck of cards, colorful handkerchiefs, and more. Ella beamed and insisted on carrying it to the front counter.

A woman with a streak of bright blue hair rang up the purchase and smiled. "Great pick. You're gonna love this kit. Come back soon and show me some of your tricks. I love a good show."

She slid the receipt at us along with a colorful flyer. "Speaking of, don't miss the one that's about to start. Vanishing Lakes' annual ice-sculpture contest, part of the festival. The sculptures are incredible. They're on display on the trail around Shadow Lake, and at the end of the evening, the town votes on a winner. It's fun for the whole family." She winked.

It did sound intriguing, but my mind snagged on her last remark. Did she think we were a family? I supposed it looked that way. A nice thought, but a false one. One I shouldn't entertain.

"Can we go, Mommy? Please? I've never seen an ice sculpture before." She paused. "What's an ice sculpture?"

Max and I laughed as we left the store. "It's like a

statue," I said, "but made of ice."

Max popped the magic kit into the car and looked at me. "What do you say? You want to go?"

If I said no, we'd return to the house, where they'd likely practice tricks and I would stress over the events of the day and worry about what might happen next. And how many opportunities were there in January to enjoy the outdoors?

I smiled. "Let's do it."

Twenty-One

"Look—it's a dragon!" Ella turned wide eyes our way before gaping again at the impressive carving complete with sharp teeth glittering in the setting sun. She kept skipping ahead to each new sculpture, always more fascinated with the next. She hadn't complained once about the cold.

"You warm enough?" Max asked me.

I nodded. "As long as we keep walking, I'll be fine. This really is amazing." Besides the dragon, we'd admired carvings of a castle, a guitar, a ship, and a penguin, each chiseled with astounding detail from massive blocks of ice supported on tables spaced out along the lakeside trail.

Max's phone buzzed for about the fifth time since we'd started walking. "Come on. Let up, already." He glanced at it with irritation. "My manager can be a real pain."

"I don't mind if you answer. Maybe it's important."

"Yeah, important like making sure I'm not breathing wrong. The guy would make a good parole officer." Max rolled his eyes. "This'll just take a minute." He put the phone to his ear. "Yeah, Brian." He lowered his voice and fell back as I continued following Ella.

A few minutes later, he caught up to me. "Well, that was obnoxious."

I almost chuckled but held it in because he didn't look amused.

Max shoved the phone in his pocket. "He heard the crowd and kept asking where I was. Almost blew a gasket when I told him." With a long-suffering sigh, Max slid on a pair of sunglasses. "Ridiculous in this light, but I told him I'd wear them."

"Should we leave? I don't want you to get in trouble. If someone recognizes you—"

"Let them." He shoved the glasses to the top of his head. "I'm not hiding like I'm some kind of criminal."

"Hot chocolate!" Ella pointed. "Can we get some?"

We followed her to the booth and Max bought three cups, one for each of us. Steam billowed. "Careful," I warned Ella, "it's super hot."

She blew on it and hurried ahead to the next carving, a small igloo.

Still sensing Max's unsettled mood, I searched for a change of subject while nestling my cup, savoring the warmth. "That was really nice of you to offer to teach Ella tricks for the show. Do you really think she'll be able to manage it?"

"Sure, it'll take practice, but she's got gumption. Like her mom. She'll do great."

I puffed a breath, vapor dissipating in the frigid air.

Me? Gumption? "Please. How many times have you seen me scared out of my wits?"

"Hey, being brave doesn't mean not being scared. It means you keep going even though you are."

Me, brave? I could almost hear Connor laughing.

"And don't forget . . ." Max leaned over to whisper in my ear, and my heart skipped. "You did pull a weapon on me."

My face flushed. "Don't remind me." I took a sip of hot chocolate, wishing I could hide my entire face in the cup.

"Hey." He nudged me playfully with his elbow. "You're not afraid to defend yourself and Ella. Be proud of that. I know I'm impressed."

I dropped my gaze. He wouldn't be if he knew how I'd let Connor push me around all those years.

I squinted off into the distance. "I don't think it was some random person in the house today. I only caught a glimpse, but . . . it looked like Connor." There, the crazy thought was out. "It even smelled like him."

Max stayed silent a moment. "Did you tell the police that?"

"I did. They seemed to think I was claiming I'd seen a ghost. They think he's dead."

Another beat of silence. "There's one way you could find out for sure. Whether he's dead or not, I mean." Max cleared his throat. "An exhumation and a DNA test. Not saying I recommend it. And you'd probably have to jump through a thousand hoops to get it done."

Such drastic measures. I shivered.

Ella's delighted squeals seemed to come from far away, though she was only several feet ahead. My brain no longer registered the ice sculptures. "I . . . I'll think about it."

If Connor was alive, why didn't he come for me and Ella? What was he waiting for?

My gaze skittered to the trees, examining shadows. What if he was watching, waiting for the right moment to snatch me? Make me pay?

I never should've brought this up. I edged closer to Max's side. What had we been talking about before all this? Ella. Practicing magic tricks.

"Thanks again for your willingness to help Ella, especially when you have your own tricks to work on." I pulled in a breath, desperate for a sense of normality. "How did you get started in magic, anyway? It's such an unusual career choice."

Max's stride slowed, his expression turning thoughtful. "My dad took me to see some fancy magic show—I don't even remember who or where. I was probably about Ella's age, maybe a little younger. The lights, the music, the tricks—they were spectacular. I'd never been so fascinated. And when I was picked to come on stage, I was so excited. Standing in the spotlight with everyone watching, cheering—Char told me she would've fainted, but I loved it."

I had no trouble imagining him just as confident as a small boy as he was now.

"After the show, the magician gave me a souvenir pin, a clunky round thing with a picture of a top hat and wand on it. I think I wore it for weeks, including when I slept." He gave a slight chuckle. "Just a cheap piece of junk, but I've still got it."

The statement touched me in a funny way as I realized he didn't mind admitting to a little sentimentality.

"That night was one of my best memories with my dad. One-on-one time with him was hard to come by. Then when he bought me some tricks and magic books, I practiced like crazy to impress him. And I discovered just how much I liked confounding people—especially Char."

His grin widened. "I made her watch all my tricks, till she started running the other way when she saw me coming with a deck of cards. She'd rather use them to play solitaire."

I laughed, picturing it, and tossed my empty cup as we passed a trash can. "You must've been a real pest, because it takes a lot to annoy her."

"Right? Patience of a saint." He rubbed his jaw. "Just one of our many differences. She hates conflict, I create it." He grimaced. "When my dad died, I didn't handle it well."

"But you were only a teenager." Sixteen, from what I recalled.

"The worst age. I thought I knew everything. My grandfather thought my interest in magic was a waste of time. He wanted me to be scholarly, to buckle down so I could run his business someday. The more he pushed, the more I resisted. All I wanted was for him to be like my dad, even in just the smallest way. But he never was. It made me so angry."

He cleared his throat and was silent for several steps. "It was my fault Charlene got kidnapped. Oh, she'll tell you it wasn't, but it was." He shook his head, lowered his voice. "Thank God she survived."

"Thank God you both did."

But Max went on as if he hadn't heard me. "I never deserved a sister like her. I think God made her that good to balance me out."

I almost stopped walking. "Don't say that, it's not true. You have lots of good in you too." Hadn't anyone ever told him that?

He shrugged. "Anyway, I used the notoriety from the kidnapping to jump-start my career. Sorry for the long-winded answer."

"I like long-winded answers." I liked hearing him talk, getting to know him on a deeper level.

"Yeah?"

"Yeah."

"Okay." He gave me an amused but appreciative glance. "Well then, I guess I'll keep going. What I really like is how something ordinary"—he lifted a coin between his thumb and finger, then made it travel easily across the backs of his fingers—"can become fascinating and put a smile on someone's face." He grinned at me, and I smiled back, the simple connection warming me.

"And you never let the success go to your head, that's pretty impressive." No, that wasn't what I'd thought when he'd first arrived, but I did now. With all my heart.

He laughed. "My grandfather would disagree, although he hardly knows me, since he disowned me years ago." His smile faded. "Plenty of people would disagree. Especially lately." He flicked the coin in the air, caught it, and pocketed it.

We walked on, our steps well matched, our hands close enough to touch. Had I moved closer, or had he? I wasn't sure.

"My parents disowned me when I got pregnant with Ella." I rarely spoke of it, hardly knew why I did now, except I felt he'd understand. And wouldn't judge.

"So they've never even met her?" He watched Ella giggling at a sculpture of a dancing duck and trying to imitate its goofy pose.

"Nope."

He let out a long breath. "They're only hurting themselves. It's their loss."

"Right? And your grandfather, he's missing out too."

Max took my hand and squeezed it, as naturally as if he'd been doing it for years, and yet there was nothing ordinary about the way it made me feel.

Like he understood me more than anyone ever had.

Like we belonged together.

The sun dipped below the tree-fringed horizon, and I admired the last lingering streaks of reddish pink. The world dimmed and the shadows stretched. Lights came on, bringing a whole new beauty to the ice sculptures.

I'd almost forgotten about the people all around us. Some hurried along the path, others lingered. Some took pictures and videos. As we fell into silence, I heard snippets of other conversations. The words "Mirror Lake" caught my attention.

"He's usually up here by now. He never misses this, but I wasn't able to get ahold of him . . ."

That was all I heard before the next sculpture came into view. Ella trotted ahead, and we had to pick up our pace. I glanced back, didn't recognize anyone, but something about the thread of conversation made me think about how isolated Mirror Lake was. The only other home I'd glimpsed was the cottage from Max's window.

"Ooh . . . look at the ice angel," Ella breathed, still several steps ahead. Lights shone on the sculpture, enhancing its shine. "It's almost as pretty as my angel."

I smiled at her reference to the wooden angel carving given to us before she was born, a reminder of God's love and care when we'd needed it the most. In my eyes, nothing could ever be more beautiful than that.

Something told me that this evening, this walk, had been just what we needed.

A few moments later, Ella reached for my hand, then Max's, breaking our hold on each other yet still connecting us. Standing there with them both, everything felt right, despite the recent turmoil.

How was it possible to feel so warm, so content, in such a cold setting?

"Max? Is that you?"

The breathless female voice made us both turn.

"Leslie." Max froze. "How did you—?" He backed up, his expression a cross between bewilderment and dread. "You can't be here."

The beautiful woman strode to his side in the most fashionable coat and boots I'd ever seen. "It's okay, Max."

His jaw tensed. "The restraining order—"

"I decided not to file it." She laid a hand on his arm. "We both said some things we didn't mean, and I'm sorry. I never wanted to hurt you. Now that we've both had some time to think things over—" She glanced at me. Worry shaded her luminous blue eyes. "Who's this?"

There was nothing unkind in her gaze, but her presence sent my nerves jumping and sparking like live electric wires.

I didn't trust myself to speak, and I'd never seen Max tongue-tied before.

Leslie glanced toward the trees. "Can we talk in private?"

Max gave a strange laugh. "You tracked me down in a crowd, so no. Plus, that didn't work out so well last time."

Hurt flickered across her lovely features. "Let's at least keep our voices down. The last thing we need is another spectacle." She moved in and spoke so close to his ear, I couldn't catch a word.

And I didn't want to. I moved forward with Ella and tried to untangle my nerves, squelch the strange sense of panic.

"Brook, wait up." Max returned to my side a few minutes later. "You didn't have to leave."

"It's okay, you had important things to talk about."

He shook his head and spoke harshly under his breath. "I can't believe Brian told her where to find me. Turns out he gave her my address a week ago. I should fire him. If he's that desperate for us to get our act back together, what's that say about his confidence in me? My ability to succeed on my own?"

He kept the worry from his tone, but I caught it in his eyes. A dark fear.

"Are you?" I asked quietly. "Going to get the act back together with Leslie, I mean."

He was silent a moment too long. "How could I? It would never feel right. Not after everything."

But I got a strange sense he was hoping I'd encourage him to.

A few steps later, he added, "She says she'd make a statement clearing everything up. Defending me."

"But only if you get back together?"

He glanced over his shoulder like that question hadn't

occurred to him and maybe he could still clarify it.

I didn't need any clarification.

Manipulation, that's what it was.

Not that it was my place to tell him, but I hoped Max could see that for himself. And was strong enough to resist. I supposed it depended how badly he wanted his reputation restored, his life of fame and fortune back.

We fell into silence, and when Ella's steps finally slowed and she fought yawns, I said, "I think it's time to call it a night." And when she didn't protest, I knew it was.

"I'm too tired to walk back," she moaned.

"How about your arms? They too tired to hold on?" Max crouched down, offering his back.

"Yay!" Ella climbed on, looking thrilled as we made our way to the car.

At the house, after a quick snack and a bath, Ella carried her book to where Max was prodding a log in the fireplace. "Do you want to read me my bedtime story tonight?"

"Do I?" He set the poker down. "I thought you'd never ask."

I tucked Ella into bed and listened as he read, and as much as I'd tired of the trite stories, I had to admit he breathed new life into them, animatedly acting out the characters' actions and voices, giving them personalities.

Ella sighed with satisfaction at the end. "Now prayers." She bowed her head. "Dear God, thank You for today and for my book and my new home, and I hope I can live here forever."

Oh, Ella.

"Please bless me and Mommy and Max. Tell Daddy I love him and that Max is taking care of us now, and I like that he's really nice." Her voice lowered to a whisper, but I still heard it. "He doesn't yell at Mommy or hurt her like Daddy used to."

My body stilled and my mouth dried. I couldn't bear to look at Max, but from my peripheral vision I saw him stiffen.

As Ella finished her prayers, emotions tore through me. With one simple statement, she'd announced my shame, my weakness.

What would Max think of me now?

Twenty-Two

To my surprise, Ella didn't demand I stay in the room with her, but I lingered after Max slipped out, my mind churning while she drifted off.

This house was a temporary place at best, and I should have made that clearer to her. She was getting way too attached.

As was I.

It wasn't Max's job to take care of us, yet she saw him as filling the hole left by her father. All the time we were spending with Max was sending the wrong message.

Max. If only I could pretend he hadn't heard her revealing words. I dreaded facing him, but hiding in here till tomorrow would only draw out my discomfort.

Entering the living room, I found him facing the fire, standing with his back to me. A thick black book hung partially open from one hand.

I cleared my throat. "I'm sorry about that. I hope you know I don't expect you to take care of us. I'll talk to Ella tomorrow and explain—"

"Did he hurt you?" He turned, his gaze intense. "Did your husband hurt you?"

My brow flickered. "You can't believe everything a child says."

"So you're saying your daughter's a liar?" He closed the book and set it on a side table.

I scowled. "Of course not. But children don't understand everything they see or hear. Adults have disagreements. Arguments. Everyone does."

"But not everyone needs to flee from their husband in the middle of the night."

"I never said—"

"You didn't have to. I figured it out."

I folded my arms. "He had a temper. It sometimes got the best of him."

Flames crackled. Heat washed over me, seeped into every pore and vein. And Max just kept staring, waiting for more.

I lifted my chin. "He tried his best. He was good to Ella. And okay to me most of the time."

"Most of the time," Max repeated, his expression unreadable. "Did he ever hit you?"

I considered telling him it was none of his business, but my tongue stuck. And my lack of reply spoke for itself.

Disgust curled his lip. "I should've known."

My nostrils flared. "Why on earth should you have known? You couldn't have. You didn't even know him."

"I knew enough." His fists clenched. "When you went back to him, I knew it was a mistake. I should've stayed in touch with you. I could've—"

"That's ridiculous." I stepped forward, indignation sparking anger. "Don't make this about you. I was never your responsibility. I made my choice. Me." I aimed a finger at my chest. "It wasn't anyone's job to rescue me from it."

His jaw hardened. "If I wasn't so busy being insulted that you chose him over me, I might've seen the warning signs. I could've helped you."

I made an exasperated noise. "No, you couldn't have."

Pain played across his features. "Why'd you stay with him so long?"

I stared into the fire. Easier to study the writhing flames than his face, which was full of disappointment that I hadn't been strong enough, smart enough, brave enough.

"I thought it was best for Ella." I clasped my hands together. "He loved her. And he always tried to make it up to me. In his own way, I think he loved me too."

Max seemed to process that with a slow blink. "Why'd you finally leave?"

"Ella," I whispered, trying to block the memory. "He usually didn't lose it when she was around. But . . . she got in the way—he hurt her." I shook my head, struggled to control my emotions.

"Then he got what he deserved."

I stepped back, my heart flinging up a shield against his harshness.

Regret flashed across his face, but not for what he'd said. "I'm sorry for everything you went through." He reached for me, his voice softer. "I'm sorry I wasn't there for you."

Tears escaped my eyes as I looked into his. All judgment and severity were gone, replaced with . . . what? Tenderness. And . . . something more. Something deeper.

My heart pinged with hope. But no, I had no business allowing such fancies, reading anything more into this than sympathy.

I pulled away. "Don't feel sorry for me. I made stupid choices. I reaped the consequences."

His eyes flashed. "You deserved better, no matter what he tried to make you think."

I struggled to keep my eyes from revealing the thick, dark webs of doubt wound so tightly around my soul I feared I'd never be free of them.

Yet I sensed he saw them—I couldn't hide the truth from him.

And so I let my gaze flow honestly over him. If only I'd made a different choice all those years ago.

"You deserved better," he repeated. "You still do. You're precious, Brook. You are." His words stunned me, yet touched me like a healing balm to my soul, dissolving the dark webs.

He drew me near, and I let him, my treacherous mind taking me down a path I had no right to go.

He stroked my hair back from my damp cheeks, his

eyes searching mine. "I admire your courage for finally leaving. I'm sorry I let you down. Us down. If I'd been less focused on myself, my pride . . ."

I tried not to realize how good his touch felt, tried not to lean into it, while every cell of my body yearned to.

"I should've flown out and convinced you not to marry him. Whatever it took. But my career always came first. I was stupid. You were worth dropping everything for." His face hovered inches from mine. "You still are."

He closed the distance between our lips, his meeting mine with a firmness that conveyed conviction, not doubt; passion, not pity, his fingertips in my hair working magic, my senses tingling with desire.

He drew me closer, but it wasn't close enough. My mind swirled, thoughts feverish. Heat overwhelmed me. We were too close—literally and figuratively—to the flames.

I was going to get burned.

Pulling away from his lips, I stumbled back from the fireplace.

My heart pounded, wanting him, but my brain screamed a warning.

Relinquishing myself into the arms of a man had only ever brought heartache. Regret.

I could tell myself Max was different—maybe even believe it—but I wouldn't just be risking myself, I'd be risking Ella. She'd been through too much already.

"I care about you, Brook." Max's gaze scorched me

with its strength, but he didn't step closer, didn't regrasp my arms. "I know this is hard for you. You've been through so much. But we can take it slow."

I shook my head. "I have to think of Ella. I have to put her first. This would be too confusing for her, too risky. If it didn't work out . . ."

And how could it? Max was a free spirit with a polar opposite lifestyle, a home in California. He was the one who'd said, *You can't tie a magician down.*

Ella needed stability. Reliability. "You heard her. She's already way too attached."

"I care about her too. You know that."

"You've known her a short time." I gave a sad laugh. "It's fun playing a role for a little bit, but the reality of life with a child—it's hard work. The hardest ever. You're on the clock twenty-four seven, whether you've slept or not. Your life isn't your own."

"You don't think I could handle that?"

"I couldn't ask you to. It's too much commitment."

Max stepped back. A shadow crossed his face, like reality hitting him. "It was just a kiss."

An amazing kiss. But to rich and famous Max, what was one more? I swallowed hard. He'd probably kissed more women than he could remember.

But even one kiss was too much for me. It came with expectations, and I had nothing left to give. Not after Connor. "I'm sorry, Max."

"Don't be. It was my mistake."

I couldn't look at him. My gaze fell on the book he'd set down earlier. A Bible. Was that what he'd been doing before I stepped into the room? Reading a Bible? And why did that surprise me?

This man was complicated. Compassionate. Confident and vulnerable. Flawed and real.

Everything I wanted.

Everything I couldn't have.

He put his hand on the book. "I don't read it enough. But when I find myself wanting a drink, I know it's time. And today's been a heck of a day."

At least we could agree on that.

Max picked up the book, and I retreated to my room just in time to let my tears fall.

We'd ruined everything.

And now I had to leave.

Twenty-Three

Sleep eluded me most of the night. I didn't want to face the day, but I dragged myself from bed when Ella woke up.

Grateful for Max's habit of sleeping late, I fed Ella and left a pan of muffins on the stove. Too bad they'd probably be cold by the time Max woke up.

I dropped Ella off at kindergarten. She was unaware of the changes we'd have to make, but I consoled myself with the fact that she wouldn't have to switch schools again as long as we stayed in Vanishing Lakes. I spent the day researching apartments, talking to a few landlords, and obtaining some applications.

After grabbing a late lunch, I waited in the school lot with a good forty minutes to spare before classes let out. I pulled out my phone and searched a topic that had weighed on me since yesterday.

Exhumation.

My stomach tightened as I scanned the daunting requirements. An exhumation license. Permission from the cemetery. And consent from the deceased's next of kin.

I'd never get that.

I lowered my phone, discouraged. Yet, in a cowardly way, relieved.

I didn't want to deal with an exhumation, but Max had made it seem like the next logical step.

Max.

I had to stop thinking about him. About his lips on mine. About his hands in my hair, stirring up feelings I couldn't handle.

Because the attraction was so much more than physical. He shared my faith, wasn't afraid to turn to God. And something about that—that deep, spiritual connection—both thrilled and terrified me.

A blast of cold air hit me, and I turned to see a man climbing into my passenger seat.

Ian.

With a gasp, I recoiled. Alarm squeezed my vocal cords. "What do you think you're doing?"

"Finally getting the truth out of you." He glared and slammed the door.

"Get out of here!" I reached for my door handle, but he seized my wrist, catapulting my heart to my throat. I pulled against his grip. "Let go!"

"You told my mom to give me a warning." He leaned close. "Consider this yours."

I bared my teeth. "Get out of my face."

His expression reflected mock amusement. "Maybe I will. Once you admit the truth about what you did."

"I already have." I channeled all the vehemence I could muster into my voice. "You just don't want to believe it."

His upper lip curled. "You're a liar. And you know what me and Connor think of liars." His hand made a fist, and I flinched.

A smile stretched his face. I had to get my nerves under control. My fear gave him way too much satisfaction.

If only he didn't remind me so much of Connor.

Except Ian's hair had grown scraggly, like he couldn't bother to cut or even groom it. His prickly chin jutted with attitude. "Either way, you're gonna lose Ella."

My heartrate spiked. With my free hand, I turned on my phone.

He knocked it from my grasp. "You think I don't know what you've been up to? Dishonoring Connor. Shacking up with that washed-up Perigard."

Heat blasted through my veins. "You don't know what you're talking about."

Angry energy radiated from him. "Didn't think anyone would find out, did you?"

I met his eyes and made my voice firm and cold as hardpacked snow. "I'm friends with his sister. I rented a room. There's nothing wrong with that." It crossed my mind to tell him I was moving. But no, I wouldn't justify myself to him. And I certainly didn't want him knowing I'd soon be living alone.

"Yeah? He gets this cozy with all his renters?" He whipped out his phone and played a YouTube video . . .

Max and me at the ice festival, hand in hand against a sunset sky.

My mouth dropped. Had Ian been there yesterday, stalking us? "We weren't doing anything wrong."

"Says you. Maybe you should read the comments, see what the rest of the world thinks." His tone couldn't have been more gloating.

"That proves nothing." I tried to slap the phone away.

He blocked me. "We'll see what the judge thinks of you putting your daughter at risk by consorting with a wild playboy."

My mind buzzed. "He's not a playboy."

"You really that naive, or just stupid?" He flashed another video, this one of Max in a crowd of some sort. A bar or a club. Drink in hand, liquid sloshing. He stood red-faced, yelling. Angry.

I barely had a moment to absorb it before Ian shoved another video in my face, this one of Max with his arms slung around two gorgeous women. Probably models or actresses.

I turned away stiffly. "Those videos are old."

"What's the difference? Don't tell me he's gone and fed you some story about being a changed man. And that you bought it." He scoffed and shoved the phone back in his pocket. "You think living with this guy makes it look like Ella's your priority?" He stuck his finger in my face. "You're losing custody. Guaranteed."

My cheeks burned.

"And then you're going to prison. Your pitiful little alibi? Won't mean a thing once a judge hears you've got a history with Perigard. He may have done the killing, but you're just as guilty."

"You're delusional."

"We'll see about that."

The school bell rang, the long electronic tone signaling freedom. On the far side of the building, a line of buses waited.

Ian released my wrist and patted my cheek. "Enjoy Ella while you can."

"Get out."

But he was already going, swaggering off through a line of parked cars.

I pressed my hands to my forehead. Pulled in deep breaths. Tried desperately to gather my wits, steady my trembling body. I couldn't let Ella see me this way.

Images from the video clips replayed in my mind. I'd overlooked too much, been a fool to think I could ignore the public side of Max's life, pretend it didn't exist, wouldn't touch us. I'd never stopped to think how my living at the lake house could be twisted into something so ugly.

I prayed it wasn't too late to fix this.

Driving back, I barely heard a word of Ella's chatter. I was too busy breathing in and out, settling my shaken nerves. And keeping an eye out for Ian.

I considered going to the police but wanted to spare

Ella the drama.

There'd be more than enough drama when I informed her we were leaving. She'd be shattered. I braced myself, preparing for a showdown.

"Max!" Ella yelled the moment we stepped inside. She dropped her coat and backpack and scampered off to find him.

"No, Ella. Come back."

I followed her to the living room, where Max stood beside the coffee table. What in the world was he grinning so widely about?

"Look what I got." With a flourish, he produced a top hat. "About time, hey?"

"Neat!" Ella said. "Can I see?"

"You bet. Better yet, I'd like you to take this"—he produced a large yellow handkerchief—"and hold the two corners. And you"—he gestured to me—"hold the other two."

Honestly, this man. Couldn't he see my agitation? Didn't he remember the sparks that had flown the last time we'd been in this room? Or did he simply create his own reality as the mood suited him?

I had serious talking to do, and here he was playing magician.

Making Ella's face shine and eyes dance with glee.

My heart panged. Fine. We'd share one more happy moment before I broke my news. I always did prefer delaying unpleasantness.

Max's face went still with concentration. "And with a wave of my hand—" He pulled the handkerchief away, and a white rabbit popped up and peered at us from inside the hat.

Ella squealed with delight, jumping up and down. "A bunny! Finally! Oh, it's so cute. What's its name?"

Max scooped up the animal, tipped the hat onto his head, and plopped the creature into Ella's arms. "Since it just appeared out of thin air, it doesn't have a name yet. You want to give it one?"

"Oh yes!" She squeezed it. "And it needs someone to love it and take care of it. Can I keep it?"

"Sure."

I cleared my throat and shot a severe look Max's way. "It's not yours, Ella. Go play with it in the front hall, but you can't keep it. Max and I are going to talk." I gestured for him to follow me, then marched into the kitchen.

Twenty-Four

"Uh-oh." Max's eyebrows hiked. "Looks like I'm in trouble." He didn't sound at all concerned. And there was that infuriating grin again.

"Honestly, Max. How could you do that?"

"What?"

"You can't just give her an animal." I put my hands on my hips. "You should've asked me first. A pet is a huge responsibility, way too much for a six-year-old."

"Come on, she's a smart kid. She can handle it once I show her what to do. It'll be good for her." He craned his neck to catch a glimpse of her. "Look at her. She's in love."

Of course she was, snuggling her face into the rabbit's fur and talking to it like it was a baby.

"And it's a rescue. I thought you'd like that. Though to be fair, I'll warn you the shelter said it's always trying to escape. Actually, I had to track it down right before you got here. But an escape-artist rabbit? I had to have it."

"Of course you did." I kept my tone even. "You have to have what you want, when you want it. But you can't fix everything with money."

His grin dropped. His eyes tightened. "You're mad about last night."

"This is nothing to do with that." I folded my arms.

"Sure it is. Don't punish Ella because you're ticked at me."

I was getting more ticked by the moment. "You don't get it, Max. It's not your place to give Ella a pet." I aimed my finger at him. "You don't get to make any decisions when it comes to her. She's my child." I poked my chest. "My responsibility. I decide what's best for her."

His lips, which I'd been trying to avoid looking at, pressed together. Something like hurt flashed across his face. "I was only trying to do something nice."

I steeled myself against my softening heart. "I appreciate that. But you should have asked. You assume too much."

"Right, I can't really read minds. And reading you— impossible." He thumped the top hat down on the table. "I'm sorry about last night. It shouldn't have happened. As for the rabbit, don't worry. I'll take care of it." He turned. "But I have to start helping her practice. That talent show's going to—"

"Max, no."

He turned back. "No? What do you mean?"

I met his gaze, mine firm. "You can't teach her magic."

He looked at me as if I'd just announced he could never eat again. "Why not?"

"Because we're leaving. We can't live here anymore."

He paused, gaze assessing me. "Because of last night? Come on, Brook. Now that I know how you feel, I promise it won't happen again. And with everything you've been dealing with, you shouldn't be on your own right now."

"I'm sorry, but I've made up my mind. We can't stay. I never should have in the first place." I should have followed my instincts and left that first night he'd arrived, despite the nice moments we'd shared—what good were they now? What did they do but make leaving harder?

He lifted his chin. "Why not?"

"Don't make me spell it out for you." Something about his silence made my tongue keep flapping. "It's just not right." Not with these feelings swirling between us, the sparks of attraction. "And it doesn't look right either."

"So you're worried about what other people think."

"It's not only that. You live a certain way." I glanced around the room and gestured with my hands. "And we don't fit into this lifestyle."

"A certain way?" He said it like I'd insulted him.

"We need a simple, quiet life. Not one in a spotlight. Because even if you're avoiding it now—you can't forever. It's waiting for you, and you want it back. It will find you, and then it finds us. I have to do what's best for Ella." It was on the tip of my tongue to tell him about Ian, but that would only make him angry. He'd insist on me staying so he could protect me.

I lowered my voice. "Her grandparents are trying to get custody. If I'm living here, they'll rip me apart in court. They'll take Ella."

He frowned, his eyes darkening. "Why? Am I some kind of monster?"

"Of course not. It's nothing personal."

He scoffed. "Of course it is."

I sighed with frustration. Why was he making this so difficult? "I've seen videos, Max. Of you. Your lifestyle and temper."

"Really? Videos?" His sarcasm rang clear. His jaw clenched. "I don't suppose it matters that those were from years ago. That I've grown up since then. Might've done it the hard way—the stupid way—but I have." He raked a hand through his hair. "And why are you so convinced that just by association with me, you'd lose Ella? You could fight that. I could help."

"I'm not going to fight an unnecessary fight, not with Ella at stake. I don't have the money, and I'm not taking yours. I'm not trying to hurt you. I just can't risk—"

"Hey, I get it. You hate risk, and I'm nothing but risk. And playing it safe has always turned out great for you. I mean, we both know you chose a real winner."

I glared at him. "That's low."

"All I'm saying is, I never would've treated you like him. Never. But you were too scared to give me a chance."

"That's not fair," I whispered.

"And another thing. No one's perfect. If you had a camera on you almost every second of your life—especially when you weren't aware of it—even you'd be caught in a few less-than-stellar moments. Unless you're a saint. Me, at least I know enough to know I'm not. Never claimed to be." He turned on his heel and stalked off.

* * *

"Mommy, where's Max?" Ella asked, the rabbit cradled in her arms.

"Don't bother him, sweetie. He's busy."

Busy being angry.

My own emotions simmered like the stew on the stove. I stirred it, swirling vegetables and beef like the thoughts in my mind. I wasn't ready for another confrontation, but I had to break the news to Ella so she had time to process it.

Max didn't show himself for the rest of the night, and I found myself wondering if he had a secret store of food downstairs. Ridiculously, I found myself hoping he did because I didn't want him going hungry. He couldn't seem to go more than a few hours without eating. Yet he somehow stayed in great shape. Must be nice to have a magic metabolism.

I stirred the stew so hard I almost splashed myself. The last thing I needed was to be mooning over Max's physique. His attractiveness was plenty clear to me, and just one of the many reasons I needed to get out of here.

"Can't Max read my story to me tonight?" Ella asked at bedtime, her eyes hopeful as she stroked the rabbit.

"No, I'm sorry." And not only that . . . I pulled in a bracing breath and settled close to her. "I know you like it here and that you like Max, but this was always just a temporary situation."

"What's 'temporary' mean?" She gave me a suspicious look.

"It means 'for a little bit.'" I continued before she could ask what "situation" meant. "What I'm trying to say is . . . we need to find our own place to live. Just you and me."

She gasped, clearly horrified. "And leave Max? Who would take care of him?"

I was struck by a strange urge to laugh and cry. Take care of him? Last night during her prayers she'd claimed he was taking care of us.

"He's a grown man. He doesn't need anyone taking care of him."

"Sure he does." She scooped up the rabbit and cuddled him. "We make sure he has fun, eats healthy food, and we pray for him."

I swallowed a lump. "Well . . ." I smoothed her hair. "He'll manage just fine. And we can still pray for him."

"But I'll miss him, Mommy. Won't you?"

"We'll be fine. We have each other." That was all that mattered.

"No." She backed away. "I don't want to go. I don't want to move again." Her lower lip protruded in a pout and her voice turned whiny. She clutched the rabbit closer. "Can I bring Frosty?"

Frosty. She'd named the creature after a snowman. If only it would melt away like one.

"He can stay in our room tonight," I said, skirting the question as I opened the cage door. "But right now, it's bedtime."

She started crying. I wasn't sure what was worse: this pitiful sound that tore at my heart, or the tantrums that drove me insane. I drew her into my arms and held her close. "It'll be okay, it'll all be okay . . ."

Twenty-Five

Ella wanted to sleep with the rabbit in bed with her, so that was another battle. Weary as I was, I expected to drop right to sleep when she finally nodded off, but my mind wouldn't let me.

Periodic little noises from the rabbit cage irked me. I longed for the temporary respite of unconsciousness. But eventually my awareness dulled, and when I groggily lifted my phone to check the time, I discovered hours had passed.

Had I dreamed or simply imagined the rabbit scampering around the room, trying to jump into our bed, its beady red eyes staring at me? I activated my flashlight app and shone the beam at the cage. I spotted the water bottle and bowl of food pellets, but no rabbit.

Hoping it had simply burrowed into the straw, I slipped from bed and found the metal door slightly ajar. No rabbit inside.

Wonderful.

I crawled around the room, peering under the bed and furniture, only to be rewarded by finding a couple of round droppings near our door. Lovely. The little critter was taunting me. Our bedroom door hung open slightly, just enough for a small rabbit to sneak through. This just kept getting better. Of all the nights for me to forget to latch it.

With a huff, I left the room and scanned the floor, my flashlight picking up another few telltale brown rabbit gifts near the basement stairs. Careful not to step on any, I padded down the stairs as if on some kind of warped Easter egg hunt.

"Where are you, rabbit?" I whispered, irritated that I was talking to thin air. I pivoted my light and it bounced into the basement bedroom. The door stood ajar wide enough to see that the bed was empty, though messy with strewn blankets.

"Max?" I called, simply to make him aware of my presence. But no response came.

I turned to the main part of the basement, which held a pool table, a weight bench, a desk, and a corner kitchenette complete with mini fridge. No sign of the rabbit, but the space was large, with plenty of boxes and hiding places for the sneaky little animal.

Below a few coats on hooks, winter boots stood on a mat near the sliding back door, and through the glass I spotted a figure standing several yards away, beside the firepit. A small glow came from the pit, just enough to illuminate the man's features. Max. What was he doing out there at this unearthly hour?

Forgetting the rabbit, I cracked the door and called

into the cold, "What's with the three-a.m. bonfire?"

He turned, his face and expression disappearing into shadow. "Beats me." He shook his head, scooped up an armful of snow, and tossed it into the firepit.

Curious and a bit disturbed, I stuffed my bare feet into boots at least two sizes too big, pulled on a huge coat, and traipsed out the door.

Max was poking a stick at sizzling, dying embers when I reached him. My too-long coat sleeves covered my fingers but didn't make them any less chilly, so I tucked my hands under my armpits. "What gives? Why aren't you sleeping?"

"Could ask you the same."

"I'd love to be sleeping, but your dear rabbit escaped again and is leaving a delightful little trail of inedible chocolate pebbles. I think it's hiding somewhere in the basement."

The bitter tang of smoke touched my senses as a waxing moon glimmered above us.

Max shifted some ash, revealing the remains of something, a curled, solid black lump, but not charcoal. He flicked it with the stick, and it fell open.

"What the . . . ?" He reached in and pulled it out gingerly.

I squinted at what looked like the remains of a wallet. The charred, melted edges of the identification hadn't completely obliterated the face on the license.

I peered closer. "Is this some kind of weird magic trick,

because I don't think—"

Wait. I knew that face.

Connor's.

My tongue tripped over itself. "How did that get here?" My voice came out raspy, as if I'd inhaled too much smoke, though only a trace remained in the air.

"No idea." Worry laced Max's tone. He dropped the wallet like it had burned him. "I just found it, same as you."

Of course he did. Of course. Deep-sleeping Max had just happened to wake up to an unattended fire burning evidence in his yard.

I wanted to believe it.

Because the alternative was unthinkable.

"Brook, please. I know what this looks like, but I'm just as confused as you." He shook his head. "I couldn't sleep, so I ended up at my desk, figuring I'd get some work done. I saw the dim glow and came out to investigate. That's it."

He glanced at me. The darkness revealed a strange shine in his eyes. Fear? Desperation? "Tell me you don't think I had anything to do with this."

In my heart? No, never.

But my mind considered the facts. Max's only link to Connor was me, and we'd only recently reconnected. Although the timing of that . . .

A wave of coldness broke over me.

Max had shown up at this secluded place to lay low

shortly after the murder.

Coincidence?

It had to be.

He was a good person. He was Charlene's brother. My . . . what? The man I'd never forgotten, who cared about me and Ella and now conflicted my heart—to put it mildly.

"Brook?" The urgency in his voice jolted me. "Why aren't you saying anything?"

I snapped out of my trance, angry at myself for allowing Ian's accusations to poison my mind even for a second. "I know you didn't do this." I swallowed hard. "Which means someone else did."

Max tensed and scanned the yard, hands fisting. "Stay here." He darted off to search the shadows near the trees, and I shivered, knowing I should hope he found the culprit, yet relieved when he returned alone, his frustration evident.

I hugged myself. "I think I know who's responsible."

"You do?" Max's incredulous gaze snapped to mine.

"Ian. He confronted me today when I was out."

"What?" Max's jaw dropped. "Why didn't you tell me earlier?"

"It wouldn't have changed anything."

"You still should've told me."

I looked at the ground.

Max touched my shoulder. "He didn't hurt you, did he?"

"No." I fingered the cuff of my coat sleeve. "But he's claiming you killed Connor for me. I think he'd do anything to prove it. I feel terrible for pulling you into this." I lowered my voice, chills snaking through me as I glanced around uneasily. "I can't help feeling like he's still out here somewhere. Watching us."

Max's face flashed anger. He spun and yelled, "Hey!" His voice echoed into the darkness, rolled over the frozen lake, and faded into the trees. "Stop harassing us and hiding, you coward. Face me like a man." His stance said he was ready and eager to fight.

I set a hand on his arm and met hard muscle. "But . . . if he wanted to frame us, why'd he leave the wallet to burn up?"

Max shook his head. "I never saw flames, just embers. He probably put the fire out right after he set it. A breeze could've rekindled it after he left. Or maybe he didn't have time to make sure it was out. Maybe I scared him away when I switched on the basement light." He poked a stick in the firepit, stirred the ashes.

"What are you doing?"

"Making sure he didn't plant anything else."

I moved closer to Max's side and tried to think logically. "So what was his plan? To call in an anonymous tip and hope the cops would search your place and find the wallet?"

"Maybe."

An even more disturbing thought hit me. "How did

he get the wallet in the first place? The police never found it. They said the killer took it . . ."

I fell silent, processing that while wind tugged my hair, the strands lashing wildly.

No wonder Ian was so desperate for the crime to be pinned on me. He'd killed his own brother.

I pressed a hand to my forehead. "But they were so close. They did everything together." I couldn't fathom such evil, and yet, I could. Both brothers had wicked tempers.

Unless . . . And why did my mind always go back to this? "Maybe they're still doing something together. Fooling us all. Maybe no one found the wallet because Connor had it all along."

Max blew out a breath. "I sure hope you're wrong."

"Me too."

We stared at the charred wallet on the ground.

"What do we do?" I asked. "Should we call it in?"

Max's jaw flexed. "I touched it. It's got my prints on it."

"You could explain. I'd back you up."

"Doesn't mean they'd buy it."

"So what do you suggest?"

He glowered. "I'm not going down for something I didn't do."

"I'm not asking you to, but we can't destroy evidence."

"It's not evidence anymore. It's tainted. We'd just be finishing what someone else started."

Snow began falling, a steady, silent stream of soft, freezing flakes. I shivered at their touch.

Max glanced at the sky, then at me, his expression unreadable. Unbearable.

I broke eye contact. "I'd better get back to Ella." I hesitated and softened my voice. "And just so you know . . . I was planning on leaving when she wakes up."

He pressed his lips together and nodded. "You should. The cops might come tomorrow. You can't put her through another ordeal like that."

My stomach sank. My timing couldn't be worse. "I'm sorry. I wasn't trying to leave you to deal with this alone. But living here . . . it's no good for any of us."

Despite my justifications, I felt terrible. "If the police show up, let me know. I'll talk to them, do whatever I can to help you. In fact"—I reached out—"I'm taking the wallet. Then when I'm settled somewhere, I'll call the detective I've been keeping in touch with and explain everything."

Max didn't look convinced, but he didn't stop me from pocketing the wallet.

Determination filled me. "I'm not going to let Ian get away with this. It's not going to be your problem, I promise." I took his hands. "You're a good man, Max. I'm sorry I've brought you so much trouble. I'm really hoping that Ian will leave you alone once I go."

Max squeezed my hands, his gaze troubled. "And what about you? Who's going to keep you safe?"

"I'll be fine." It was time I learned to take care of myself. "I'll be careful, I promise." I eased my hands away, the simple action tearing me up inside. "Thanks for everything."

He swallowed noticeably. "Where will you go?"

"I'll figure something out."

Unsettled by how much I wanted to stay, I made myself turn and walk away.

Twenty-Six

"No, I'm not going! I'm staying here. With Frosty and Max." Ella glared at me from the other side of the bed, her entire frame rigid, radiating defiance. "And where is he? What did you do with my bunny?"

"It's not your bunny, and it's downstairs with Max. They might be sleeping. Like I said, it's time to go." Having already loaded our other few bags, I slid my backpack on and tried taking Ella's hand with my free one.

"No!"

"Gabriella Elizabeth Morton, you're coming with me right now and that's all there is to it."

Her face scrunched angrily. "I don't want to!"

As if life was determined by what we wanted. She had so much yet to learn.

I scooped her up, careful of her angry arms and flailing legs. She kicked and screamed as I wrestled her into her booster seat and buckled the belt.

I closed the door and hit the child locks, ludicrously feeling like a kidnapper. "I'm sorry, but this is what's best for us. Someday you'll understand."

"No, I won't! This is stupid."

I turned on the engine and eased out of the driveway into the early morning light. Her protests continued down the road.

"I'm unbuckling! And if you get in an accident, I'll fly out the window and then you'll be sorry!"

A distinct click made my muscles tense. "Buckle up right now, young lady." With the snow falling thickly and slicking the roads, her dire prediction could become a possibility. I scanned for a place to pull over. Where was the shoulder? I braked gently, and my heart skipped as we slid. I fought to correct it.

"I hate you! I hate you!" Ella's feet pounded my seat. My mind pulsated wildly, like the windshield wipers frantically beating the snow but losing the battle. I clenched my teeth. We'd arrived in a snowstorm and were leaving in a snowstorm. Was there a lesson in that? A warning? Besides the obvious one, beware of Wisconsin winters?

With relief, I spotted the public-access lot for Mirror Lake and pulled off the road.

"I want Max!" Ella cried. "Let me talk to him on your phone."

I hauled in a deep breath and tried to sound reasonable, when all I wanted was to match her screams. "Only if you calm down."

Amazingly, she did. So I dialed and handed her the phone.

"He didn't answer," Ella wailed.

Just my luck. He was probably sleeping.

Her cries resumed, until she swallowed a sob. "Dane. I want to talk to Dane."

Did I still have his number? I scrambled to find it. I'd never intended to call him, but it wasn't a bad idea. He'd always been able to make her smile. "Here." I dialed, then handed the phone to her and prayed he'd answer.

"Hi, Dane, this is Ella," she said in a pert voice. "I'm mad at Mommy."

Nice start. I tapped the wheel. Heard Dane's muffled voice.

"In the car," Ella said. "Just parked on the road. She's taking me to a new place to live. *Again*. And I don't want to go. I want to go back to Max's house and my bunny. And he's supposed to teach me magic tricks for the talent show." A pause. Ella let out a little laugh. "No, not the bunny. Max. Bunnies can't teach anything."

A longer pause followed, and I wished I could hear Dane's words, but after a little while, Ella thrust the phone back at me. "He wants to talk to you."

At least she wasn't crying anymore. "Hi, Dane." I tried to keep the weariness from my voice.

"So if I deciphered all that correctly, you left Perigard's place?"

I turned on kids' songs, hoping Ella would focus on that more than my conversation. "Yes."

"Based on what the Mortons have been saying about

him, I can't say I'm not relieved. But I'm sorry Ella's upset. Is there anything I can do?"

"You helped just by talking to her, so thanks for that."

"Why'd she say you're on the side of the road?"

"We're not. It's a lake-access parking lot." As if that was much better. "I pulled off till the visibility gets better. It's snowing hard."

"You're just going to sit in your car and wait? That could be a while."

True. I'd been desperate to leave and hadn't thought this through. "It might not be. Anyway, we're not far from Max's. We could easily walk back if we had to."

Dane made a disapproving noise. "Don't do that. I'll swing by and pick you up."

"Swing by? But you're hours away."

"I would be if I were in Bloomington, but I'm not." He paused. "Ian told me he confronted you. He wouldn't say when he was coming home, so I got concerned and drove up to make sure he wasn't bothering you."

"Really?"

"You don't have to sound so surprised. I told you I wanted to help. I wish you would've reached out to me sooner."

My thoughts raced. "So were you with him last night?"

"Yeah, we were ice fishing till late."

"How late?"

"I don't know. Ten? Eleven? Why?"

"And then what? Did he go anywhere after that?"

"He decided to head home." His tone turned troubled. "Why, did something happen?"

"I was just wondering. So why are you still here?"

"I figured I'd make the trip worthwhile, stay a few days and do some more fishing. Now I'm glad I did. Just tell me where you're at and I'll head out."

"You don't need to come out in this weather."

"Hey, I wouldn't ice fish if a little weather bothered me. Plus, my truck's a beast. It handles snow with no problem. Come on, I want to help. You've gotta know that by now."

I did, yet I'd always brushed him off. Maybe it was time I didn't.

When the call ended, I stared at the fluffy white stuff, so deceptively delightful. I'd ended up accepting his help because I knew it would make Ella happy. "Dane's going to come pick us up."

When that didn't elicit the expected thrilled response, I turned.

And saw an empty seat.

"Ella?"

Baffled, I scanned the floorboard. But there was nowhere for her to hide. I even checked under the passenger seat, impossible as it would've been for her to fit in the tiny space—let alone climb there without me noticing.

Apprehension clogged my throat. I threw open the door. "Ella!" My cry bounced over the road and disappeared into the snow-flocked trees. Surely if she'd simply stepped outside for a moment, she couldn't be far. How had I not noticed?

I circled the vehicle, still calling, and even checked under it. Yes, she'd been angry, but to wander off alone into a vast wilderness? The girl who wanted to hold my hand in the grocery store?

It was like she'd simply vanished.

Stopping in my tracks, I realized that by scrambling around the car I'd already obliterated any possible footprints. But when I scanned the distance, I spotted a trail of tiny prints heading back the way we'd come, though the rapidly falling snow was filling them in.

Relief changed to nervous incredulity. Where in the world did she think she was going?

Then it struck me. *We could walk back to Max's if we had to.*

Oh, Ella. I imagined her hopelessly lost while traipsing blindly through thick snowfall and vicious wind.

I had to find her.

Twenty-Seven

"Ella!" Calling for her, I followed her prints until I lost them in a stretch of wind-blown snow. Close as I was to Max's now, I raced to his driveway, trying not to grow more frantic with each step.

She had to be here. Surely I'd spot her at any moment. Surely my panic was unwarranted.

I pounded on the front door. Waited longer than I could stand.

Was Max sleeping? The thought infuriated me. Even if Ella did come here, she likely wouldn't have gotten in.

She could be hiding. She'd have to know she shouldn't have snuck away, that I'd be upset.

I cupped my mouth and yelled, "Ella, I'm not mad. I'm worried about you. Please come back!"

Snowflakes pelted me as I circled the house, peering under bushes and behind trees.

In the backyard, I made my way to the frozen shore, glanced across the expanse of snow-coated ice, then at the distant neighbor's cottage and the tangled overgrowth along the shore. No sign of Ella.

I turned back, dread deepening the pit in my stomach,

and faced the towering pine closest to the lake. The one with heavy branches swooping low to the ground. She'd hidden there the day we went sledding. I hadn't checked that yet.

I hurried to it and parted the branches.

Stifled a scream.

A man's body lay face down near the tree trunk. Sparse gray hair. Bare wrinkled hands, fingers curled.

Deathly pale.

My stomach dropped like an ice block.

I gasped and stumbled back, even momentarily forgetting Ella.

A dead body, carelessly concealed on Max's property. Horror filled me. My heart thudded with terrifying force.

"Brook!"

I whirled to see a figure approaching.

Dane. Concern swept his face as he jogged toward me. "What's up? You weren't at your car, didn't answer your phone. I figured—" He stopped short at my side. "Hey, you okay?"

I shook my head.

His gaze followed my shaky hand. I nudged the branches aside while turning away, not wanting to see the terrible sight again, but the damage was done. I couldn't unsee it.

Dane swore and stumbled back, bumping me. He clasped my arms, bracing himself as much as me. "What the—" He bit off another curse. "What happened?"

"I-I was looking for Ella, and . . ." I closed my eyes briefly, my stomach rolling, nausea rising.

He stared at me, slightly pale, and swallowed. "Who is it?"

"I don't know."

Clenching his jaw, Dane reached for the branch.

"Don't!" I grabbed his arm.

He nodded, backed up, and wiped his hands down his pants as if they were sweating. "All right, okay." He exhaled through his teeth. "I'm assuming you didn't call the police yet?"

I shook my head.

"We need to do that." He glanced at the house, his worried expression intensifying and his voice dropping. "This Perigard's place? Where is he?"

As if on cue, the basement door slid open and Max appeared in the entrance. "Hey! You looking for Ella? She's here!"

I almost fell to my knees in the snow. "Thank God."

Dane stiffened and supported my weight with his arm, then eased me forward, tension radiating from him. "Hey," he whispered, "don't let him know what you found. We'll grab Ella and get out of here as fast as we can."

The warning in his tone slowed my steps. "You think—? No, it wasn't Max."

"Let the police decide that. Please," he added with a touch of desperation. He didn't know Max like I did.

But neither did the police.

First the wallet, now this.

How was I going to tell Max?

At the basement door, I looked past him to Ella playing on the basement rug with the bunny. Her coat and boots lay discarded on the floor. "Oh, Ella, how could you run off like that? I was so worried."

"Well, I was worried about Frosty. I *told* you, Mommy."

Max, in sweatpants and a rumpled T-shirt, rubbed his mussed hair. The darkness underscoring his eyes suggested he needed rest. I wondered if he'd stayed awake long after I'd gone back to bed, then finally fallen asleep only a short time ago. I noticed a scattered assortment of small tools on his desk that hadn't been there earlier.

His voice drew my attention back to him. "She showed up several minutes ago, banging on the basement door."

"Because," Ella said, "you didn't answer the front one."

"And then we were searching for the rabbit." Max stifled a yawn. "Found it hiding in the darkest, farthest corner of the basement, chewing on a box. I tried calling your phone."

I felt my pockets. "I must have left it in my car. We pulled over a little way up the road because of the snow."

I was a coward, using small talk to delay breaking awful news. But how was I going to tell Max about the body without Ella overhearing?

Dane cleared his throat, his eyes conveying urgency and the belief we should be racing out of there. For all he knew, we were in the lair of a murderer.

"Hey there, I'm Max." He extended his hand to Dane, who almost flinched.

A ridiculous urge to laugh hit me.

"Dane." Belatedly, he accepted Max's hand and they shook. "Brook called me for a ride because of the snow."

I noticed an almost imperceptible tightening around Max's eyes. He nodded and flicked a glance my way that left me feeling I'd disappointed him.

Which was nothing compared to what was coming.

He closed the still-open basement door on the frigid wind.

Dane, who'd been glancing around uncomfortably, stepped forward and caught the handle. "We'd better get going."

Max glanced outside. "It's still snowing hard. Why don't you stay for some coffee and breakfast?" He elbowed me lightly. "I'll even make it."

"If that means ramen noodles, I think we'll pass." I smiled weakly.

"Aw, give me some credit. I can fry up some great bacon when I've got it." He paused, leaned slightly my way, and spoke from the corner of his mouth. "Do you know if I do?"

"Thanks, but don't bother," Dane said firmly. "We're

heading out. My truck cuts through snow like nothing." He turned to me, brisk and businesslike. "Let's go."

"Where're you headed?" Max asked.

"I'm not sure," I answered truthfully, while Dane shot me a warning look.

"Don't leave without the rabbit," Max said.

The rabbit? "Oh no you don't." I shook a finger. "You're the one who got that creature. You're stuck with it. The last thing I need—"

"But look at her." He gestured to Ella and lowered his voice. "You really going to tear her away from it again? It'll make the change easier on her."

"Please, Mommy?" She squeezed the rabbit with a hug so tight, I almost thought it might eliminate the issue.

Max lifted the cage. "I'll give you this, and food, and all the other stuff you'll need. And hey, check out this cool new collar I just—"

"Coming, or not?" Dane cut in, clearly more irritated than anything now. He opened the door and stepped out.

Reality returned, hitting me like the swoosh of cold air. "Fine, we'll take the thing. Ella, follow Dane."

As she trailed after him, I grabbed Max's arm and spoke in a rapid whisper. "Listen, there's something I have to tell you, and it's bad."

He gave a half-hearted smile. "Worse than you leaving?"

"Max, I'm serious." I squeezed his arm, met his eyes with regret, and forced out the words. "There's a dead body hidden under a tree in your backyard."

Max thumped the cage to the ground. Color drained from his face. "You're serious?"

I nodded, anguish piercing me. "I just found it, and Dane's going to call it in."

Disbelief swam in Max's eyes. "Who is it? Do you—"

"Shh." I motioned to Ella lingering just outside the open door, then stepped farther back into the basement, pulling him with me. "I don't know. Some poor old man, but I've never seen him before."

"Brook, come on."

I turned to see Dane had joined Ella at the door.

"Just grabbing the rabbit stuff," I said in a chipper voice. Max, his body rigid, hefted the cage.

"I'm sorry, Max. So sorry." I bit my lip. "I should stay."

"You can't." The stubborn set of his jaw told me there was no room for arguing. "Get Ella out of here."

"But—"

"Go."

By the time we loaded the rabbit, supplies, and Ella into the truck, I could see the artery in Dane's neck pumping madly.

But Dane wasn't the one I cared about.

With my eyes, I tried to tell Max I'd be back as soon as I could as Dane drove us away, but the snow clouded the space between us, and then he was gone.

"I'm glad we're out," Dane said in a low voice, his

knuckles white on the wheel. "If he knew what we saw..."
He shook his head, clearly believing we'd narrowly escaped a killer.

Whereas I believed I was abandoning a good man.

The best.

He deserved so much better than what I was leaving him to face.

Twenty-Eight

"Look at Frosty's new collar. It has his name on it," Ella said proudly.

I made myself glance at the thing, unimpressed by the rather bulky metal tag. Had Max made it himself?

"Very nice, Ella." I tried to sound like I meant it.

While she chatted with her new pet, Dane cleared his throat. He lowered his voice to an almost imperceptible level as he pulled into the lake-access lot. "I'll make the call while I get your luggage, so she won't overhear." He flicked his chin Ella's way.

I nodded and watched his serious expression through the swirling snow as he spoke into his phone while transferring our few bags into his truck.

"It's done." He climbed back in and pulled in a deep breath, as if a heavy load had just lifted from his shoulders.

Too bad it dropped onto mine.

I gripped my hands and squeezed my knuckles. "Max isn't responsible for what we found, just so you know," I said quietly. "I'm not just saying that because I trust him, but also because he wouldn't be so stupid as to—"

"Mommy," Ella piped up in a singsong voice. "You used that word."

I had to stop and think a moment to realize what she was referring to. *Stupid.*

"Yes, well, focus on yourself, young lady. After running away like you did, you're on thin ice. That was dangerous and inconsiderate. No dessert for you tonight."

"That's not fair!"

"Ella." I turned sharply and gave her a severe look. "That's enough. If you're going to keep that rabbit, you're going to have to learn to be responsible and re-spectful. And obedient."

"So where to?" Dane asked.

"A motel is fine."

"It'll have to be one that allows rabbits." He tapped the wheel as if unsure we'd find such a place. "They're like goats, always chewing on random things—furniture, wires, you name it." He glanced over his shoulder at Ella. "Careful it doesn't bite your finger." Under his breath, he muttered, "What was that guy thinking?"

He was thinking of how much Ella wanted one, and that had precluded everything else.

"Anyway, as I was saying, Max wouldn't be so *unwise* as to so carelessly try to hide such . . . incriminating evidence on his property."

"Mommy, what's 'incriminating' mean?"

The corner of Dane's mouth lifted. "I've always admired

her healthy curiosity. But why don't we discuss this later?"

I sighed and nodded. Yet a few seconds later, I added, "I just hate to think what might end up happening. What if the police jump to conclusions? He doesn't deserve—"

"Hey, not your problem. If he's innocent, he'll be fine. That's how it works."

"That's how it's *supposed* to work. If it works right. I don't have much confidence in the system right now. Not like they ever solved Connor's—" I stopped myself.

Dane nodded, solemn. "They still could. You ever call to check their progress? The cops need to know you still want answers. It keeps them from slacking."

"I have. They haven't had much to tell me. It's still an open case, but no leads." At least none I knew of. Perhaps they did have something and just couldn't tell me yet. I hoped so.

Because all they'd get at Max's would be false leads.

Wind rushed past the truck, its howl the only sound for several minutes.

We entered town and neared a motel strip.

"Shoot." Dane scowled and sped past without turning in.

"What?"

"You didn't see him?"

I craned my neck. "No, who?"

"Good." Dane released a slow breath. "Then maybe he didn't see you." He shook his head, looking baffled.

"He said he was going back to Bloomington."

Everything became clear. "Ian," I said quietly, my skin prickling.

"Ian," Dane repeated. "He lied to me."

"Does that really surprise you?" I lowered my voice. "I think he's the one trying to frame Max."

Dane glanced at me. "You're not serious."

"It makes the most sense. And you said yourself he can be crazy."

"Yeah, well, he lost his brother. He's entitled to a little anger, a little resentment. But . . . what you're saying—" He shook his head. "No, no way. You're way off the mark. I know him too well."

And I know Max.

Dane pressed his lips together. "Well, you can't stay at that motel." He slowed and pulled out his phone, his gaze bouncing from the road to his screen. "If he's still trying to hassle you, we'll have to skip the obvious places in town."

A few moments later, he turned his phone my way. "What about something like this?" He showed me a small green cottage surrounded by trees. "It's outside of town, but not too far."

I nodded. "That could work."

"It might not be available at such short notice, but I'll check."

A brief, friendly conversation later, Dane hung up, clearly pleased. "We're lucky it's the off-season."

He thumbed some information into his phone. "It's all yours."

"Just like that?"

"Just like that. Gotta love Airbnbs."

We left the town streets for a country road, and I started worrying. "How much is it per night?"

When he told me, I nodded, keeping my concern hidden.

"I took care of the first two nights." Dane turned the wheel and rumbled around a forested bend. "If you like it enough to stay longer, all you have to do is call."

I took out my wallet, but he waved it away. "No, don't worry about it."

I wasn't sure what to reply, only knew I wasn't comfortable being more indebted to him than I already was. We wound up the snow-blanketed road and approached a squat, dark green cottage covered in rough cedar shingles. Practically a shack compared to Max's place.

Not that I had any business comparing the two.

"You've done enough," I said. "This is too much."

"Yeah?" He chuckled. "Wait'll you see the inside. I didn't show you those pictures."

I let out a small laugh as I peeked at my remaining cash. "I'm sure it's fine. I appreciate all your help, but I'm not letting you pay." I held out the money.

"Suit yourself." He shrugged and took it, then parked under a carport heavy with snow, barely tall enough for his truck. I stepped out as he hurried around to my side.

"I'm hungry," Ella said, unbuckling. "Do they have sugar cereal here?"

Dane laughed. "Let's go look." He took her hand and backpack.

"Don't forget Frosty," she said. "He doesn't like the cold."

"No?" Dane shot me an amused look before grabbing the cage. "And with a name like that. What a shame."

I followed them, slogging through the snowdrifts to the little front porch, where Dane punched in the door code.

We stepped into a tidy little living space dominated by wood paneling and dull green carpet. But it sealed out the icy air and offered a cute fireplace.

While Dane built a fire, Ella followed me as I finished walking through the cottage, which took only a moment. A small kitchen, two tiny bedrooms, and one bathroom completed the place. "It's so little," Ella said.

"It's all we need." I switched on the TV. With any luck, she'd be occupied so Dane and I could really talk.

She settled on the carpet with her bunny close beside her. Dane and I sat with mugs of coffee at the kitchen table, my thoughts consumed by Max. Had the police arrived? Were they searching his house as well as his property?

Had they arrested him?

"You look worried."

I clasped both hands around the mug. "Max isn't a criminal. Someone's trying to frame him."

And I still hadn't shaken the feeling it was Ian. Maybe even Connor.

It would be the ultimate revenge—hurt the man I love.

My mind sputtered at the thought.

The man I love?

"So you think he was framed," Dane repeated, tapping his mug. "I'm not saying that's impossible, but are you sure your feelings aren't clouding your judgment?"

My feelings. Perhaps they couldn't be trusted, but that didn't change the fact that Max was innocent.

"He wouldn't hurt anyone." I forced my thoughts back to logic. "Someone's trying too hard to throw suspicion on him. So the police won't look for the real culprit." It was on the tip of my tongue to bring up Ian again, no matter how much Dane didn't want to hear it.

Dane's gaze softened. "You always think the best of people, Brook." His hand touched mine. "I'm not saying the guy plotted anything—he could've just lost it, lashed out."

He shifted in his chair, glanced over at Ella still occupied with TV and Frosty. Paused like maybe he wasn't going to keep speaking, but he did. "Why are you so sure he couldn't have done it? Because he was nice to you?"

"Because I know him."

"Maybe not as well as you think. Maybe you never saw

his angry side. Doesn't mean he doesn't have one. Most people do if you hit the right nerve. And a guy like him . . . Doesn't he have some kind of messed up, traumatic past?"

I stiffened. "Don't we all, in some way? By that line of reasoning, then even I might have done it. Maybe Connor finally hit my last nerve."

Dane stilled, his eyes turning wary.

Why had I said that? It made me sound guilty. Was I so desperate to throw suspicion off Max that I'd throw it on myself?

"I thought we were talking about the old man." Dane slid his coffee aside. "But come to think of it . . . Perigard did know Connor."

"Not really. Only slightly. Through me." I sipped my coffee, too bitter for my liking, but needing the warmth and caffeine.

"Right . . ." His brow scrunched like he was remembering something. "Connor once said you chose him over Perigard." Eyes widening, he leaned forward. "Which is a motive for Perigard to hate Connor. Hold a grudge. Maybe even—"

"No, it wasn't like that. We were never serious. Max could've had his pick of any girl. He wasn't hung up on me. He moved on easily."

Dane's brows arched. "What if he didn't?"

Wind shrieked past the small windows, emphasizing the outrageous question.

"What if that's just what he wanted you to think? He's a magician, right? An expert at fooling people. He could've been keeping an eye on you all these years, biding his time, waiting for the perfect moment to strike."

I made a disgusted noise. "That's ridiculous."

"Yeah?" Dane's eyes narrowed and he leaned back. "You gonna sit there and swear to me there hasn't been anything going on between you two these last couple of weeks?"

I avoided his eyes. Discomfort swelled my chest.

"He had you right where he wanted you." He aimed a finger at me. "We got you out just in time. You can't think badly of him or see clearly because he still has you under his spell."

I tamped down rising anger. "So if everything was going his way, why would he kill some random old man and toss him under a tree in his backyard?"

"Who knows? He might not have been random to him, and that spot was probably only temporary till he got a chance to dispose of the body properly. Thank God you came across it."

"About that." I frowned, inclining my head. "I discovered it, and you called it in. Didn't the police want us for questioning? Don't they need to take our statements?" And why hadn't this occurred to me earlier?

Dane glanced at Ella, now dancing her dolls around the living room. "Sure, but I made the call quickly and anonymously. I was trying to save you from involvement. It's not like we know anything else."

"What if we do, and we don't realize it?"

His face flushed and he scooted his chair back. "That's what you think? Okay, pack up Ella and we'll head to the station right now." He stood. "Come on, let's do it."

I opened my mouth.

Closed it.

"That's what I thought." Dane sat back down.

I stared at the table. "Do you think they'll arrest him?"

"Sure hope so."

I couldn't help shooting him a glare. "They don't have enough. It's circumstantial."

"They have a body. Criminals get convicted on less than that. And once they connect the fact that he knew Connor, it should become clear he's guilty of that murder too. It had to be someone who knew him."

I was silent a moment. "Why?"

"Because the killer didn't just kill him, he did it viciously, hatefully, stabbing him fourteen times, when once or twice would've been enough. Obvious overkill. That's a crime of passion. And crimes of passion are always personal."

I stared at Dane, his words replaying in my mind. Fourteen times. I clutched my middle, tried not to imagine Connor's blood draining from his wounds. Fourteen.

He couldn't have survived that.

What a brutal way to go.

But something else about the number churned my stomach, made it drop.

"How . . . how do you know how many times he was stabbed?"

"I found him, remember? Me and Ian." Dane closed his eyes briefly as if bracing himself against the terrible memory.

Part of me wanted to drop the subject. Part of me felt cruel for prodding, but I had to. "You could tell from that?" Surely they hadn't sat there and counted the wounds before calling for help. Or after. Who would examine such a horrendous sight longer than necessary?

He nodded. "Anyway, the police revealed that information. You're telling me you didn't know?"

I stared at him.

"My gosh." Dane's eyes widened. "I'm a jerk." He dragged a hand down his face. "I wouldn't have thrown that out there if I'd known. I'm sorry, what a way to find out." He hurried to my side. "You okay? You wanna go lie down or something?"

I stood, stepped away. "No. No, I'm good." I forced a smile. "I think I just need to think about something else. Spend time with Ella." My mind whirling, I crossed to her side and heard her say something about a dance party.

With a sigh, Dane stepped back to the table. A few minutes later, he opened his laptop. While he tapped away on his keyboard, I slipped into the bathroom, closed and locked the door. I crossed to the farthest wall and placed a call, keeping my voice as quiet as possible.

"Hello, may I speak to Detective Bale, please?"

My call was transferred, and she answered.

"Hi, Detective. Brook Morton here. I have a question about my husband's murder. Could you tell me . . . how many times was he stabbed? And was that information ever released to the public? Or even to any family or friends?" I swallowed a huge lump and waited, my heart pounding painfully.

"No, that information wasn't released. Why do you ask?"

I pulled in a sharp breath, and someone snatched my phone away.

I whirled to see Dane standing behind me, turning my phone off. His face creased into a frown while his eyes pierced me.

"Oh, Brook, why'd you have to go and do that?"

Twenty-Nine

D ane dropped my phone on the floor and crushed it with his boot. The splintering sound sent shards of fear through me.

"I don't understand." I stood with my back to the wall. He blocked the door. "You were his friend. His best friend. How could you—"

"It's not like I wanted it to happen." His face turned grim. "I didn't plan it." He reached for me, but I shrank away. He looked offended. Hurt, even. "Don't be scared. If you'd just let me explain—"

"What're you doing?" Ella walked in. "I'm bored. Can we play a game?"

My heart stuttered, and I rushed to her, encircled her in my arms. My gaze jumped to Dane, fear flipping to anger. He wouldn't dare hurt Ella, would he?

But he was a killer.

He was capable of anything.

"Sure, honey." My voice came out too raspy. "Let's play hide-and-seek. Dane will count to fifty, and we'll hide."

He gave a short laugh and nudged the broken phone

out of sight with his boot. "Nice try, Brook. But I'm not stupid."

"That word again!" Ella planted fists on her hips. "Why does everyone get to say it but me?"

"Righto, kiddo. I've gotta watch what I say." Dane's smile tightened. "Let's all go sit at the table and play a nice game of cards. How's Go Fish sound?" Dane ruffled her hair, and I wanted to smack his arm away. How dare he touch her.

But Ella could not know the truth. Ignorance would be the only thing keeping her safe.

Mindlessly, I played the game, an endless, tedious torture. I had so many questions about the murder and Dane's deception. What was going through his mind?

Ella and I had to get out of this place as soon as possible. When Dane's gaze was on his cards, I scanned for his keys. If I could get Ella into the truck, I could drive us to safety.

Fleeing on foot was the only other option, and a poor one. All I saw out the little windows were trees and snow. Isolated wilderness. No telling how far we'd have to trek, and how easily he'd probably track us down.

But how could I not try now that I knew his terrible secret? A secret he'd surely kill to keep, considering what it was. What was another murder when he'd already taken a life? Or two. He was probably responsible for the old man's death as well.

When Dane said he'd be right back and stepped into

the bathroom, my pulse ratcheted up. Could our escape be this simple?

"I have a new game," I whispered to Ella, finger to my lips. "We have to be super quick and quiet." I grabbed our coats. Stuffed my feet in boots. Made Ella do the same. Eased open the door and held the handle so it wouldn't click when I shut it.

"Climb on." I lowered myself so Ella could ride piggyback. Then I raced—as best I could—through thick snow, heading for trees, anything that could possibly shield us from view. Snowflakes spattered my face like a blast of chilly spray.

"Weee! We're going so fast, Mommy!"

"Shh!" My heart galloped with my steps, but my legs plodded. I didn't feel fast. The snow slowed me like thick mud, and Ella's weight didn't help.

A figure jogged up alongside me as if it took no effort. "Found you." Dane grinned and waved. "Come on, let's go back."

I kept moving forward.

"Hey, Ella," Dane said, "how about some hot chocolate? If you come back, I'll make you some."

"Yay!" Before I could stop her, she was sliding down my back.

I turned to see Dane tossing her in the air, then depositing her on his shoulders. "All right! You can help make it."

I glared at him. He needed no further tactics to make

me return. I would never leave Ella.

And that's what was going to make escape impossible.

* * *

"We need to talk," Dane said as Ella sipped her hot chocolate. But her eyes and ears were focused on us. "Ella, why don't you go watch some TV?"

"I'm sick of that." Almost like she knew we had something interesting to discuss.

I eyed the small bathroom. "Tell you what, Ella. How would you like to take a warm shower when you're done with your hot chocolate?" I'd never let her use the shower at home, always afraid she wouldn't wash well. A trivial concern now.

"Really?"

"Really. There's no bath here, and I think you're old enough." And most importantly, the noise would ensure she wouldn't overhear our conversation.

Once she was situated, I closed the door and faced Dane. "When she's done, I expect you to take us back to town." I spoke authoritatively, confidently, willing it to work.

He sighed and dropped onto the sofa. "Brook, come on. You know I can't do that."

"Then what, Dane?" I tried to keep desperation from my voice. "What's going to happen to us?" I glanced at the closed bathroom door, tried to block the horrible thoughts invading my mind. "She's just a little girl. I thought you cared about her."

"I do." He leaned forward, his expression earnest. "That's just it—I care about you both. Which is why you need to let me explain what happened. Once you know, you'll understand, and we can work this out. It'll be okay."

I couldn't fathom how that could be, but our time was limited. I crossed my arms. "Go ahead, I'm listening."

"I never wanted to hurt Connor. He was my best friend. But that didn't stop me from realizing what a jerk he could be. Especially to you. I hated that, Brook. I really did." He rubbed his knuckles, almost seemed nervous.

"I only wanted to help you. Sometimes I drove by your place just to make sure you were okay."

I imagined him parked in shadows, watching the house. Like a stalker. Unease prickled my arms.

"That night, I swung by on my way home and saw you leaving with Ella. It was so late, I knew something wasn't right. So I followed you."

I recalled how I'd thought I was being tailed.

"But then I lost you. I had to know what was going on, so I went back to the house. Woke Connor up." He pressed his palms against his knees, swallowed and stood.

"I'd seen him mad before, but when I told him you'd left with Ella—wow. He lost it."

Dane turned, took a few steps to the table, then paced back. I spotted his phone poking out of his back pocket.

"I couldn't get him to calm down. He brought up his

tracking app, started heading for his gun safe. Swore he was gonna kill you."

My body went rigid. I didn't even blink.

Dane clenched his fists. "We were in the kitchen. The knives were right there. When he turned, I grabbed one." He looked past me, like he saw it happening again. "And I stopped him."

He met my eyes. "I did it to save you."

Thirty

I struggled to find my voice. "So he really is dead."

"He is."

That fact settled into my brain with a cold finality.

"He can't hurt you anymore."

"I don't understand . . ." I softened my voice, ignored the rising sickness. "Why didn't you just let him leave so you could call the police?"

"And risk them being too late?" A muscle flickered in his jaw. "No way. I couldn't risk that. Couldn't risk you." He held my gaze with a burning intensity. "I've always cared about you, but I never realized until that night just how much. I'd do anything for you, Brook. Anything." The fervor in his voice pulsated in my ears.

"Then let's go to the police now. It's not too late. I'll help you explain."

His face darkened. "No one would buy that. He was stabbed in the back. Fourteen times. Once I started, it took everything in me to stop."

Overkill, a crime of passion. His words.

"And it is too late. I messed with the scene. I wiped the knife clean. Broke the back window. Did what I could to make it look like an intrusion, a robbery gone wrong. Those aren't the actions of someone acting in self-defense." He moved closer. "But I'd do it again. For you."

Why did he have to keep saying that? And what was that in his eyes? Something desperate. Hungry.

"Please tell me you understand." His muscles tightened like his life depended on my response.

I swallowed rising bile. If I pretended to understand, would it help my chances of escaping? "Now that you've explained it . . . I can see how you really had almost no choice." I wet my lips. "I know how Connor's rages were. It must have been awful."

He nodded. Seemed to be waiting for more. Hoping for more.

I took a step closer, my mind returning to his phone. "Thank you for protecting me." I leaned in to hug him, avoiding his eyes, afraid he'd see the truth, that I loathed touching him.

His arms closed strongly around me. Possessively. Like Connor's. My skin crawled. I tried not to stiffen and resist.

He exhaled, his breath fluttering my hair. "Ever since that night, I was afraid you'd figure out it was me. Part of me wanted you to, but I knew you needed time." He stroked my hair. "It drove me crazy that you left town after the funeral. But now here you are with me. Finally."

My fingertips brushed the top of his phone. "I think . . ." I slipped it from his pocket in one swift, light motion, then held my breath and leaned my head against him, distracting him. "I think you were very brave."

My pulse skipped. Had I gone too far? Could he see through my awful simpering? While my left hand pressed against his back, my right one maneuvered the phone down my palm and into my sleeve. My own awkward attempt at sleight of hand.

"Brook." He said my name with a longing that froze my blood. "As long as we're together, we can make this work."

Phone safely in my sleeve, I pressed my fingertips against the fabric, discreetly holding it shut. I eased back to look at him. Struggled to keep my anger and fear from showing. If he'd kept an eye on me before Connor's death, what lengths had he gone to after? Had he followed me to Vanishing Lakes? Was he responsible for the emails and messages?

But calling the police was all I could focus on right now. "I'm sorry . . . Just let me check on Ella, then we can talk some more."

I stepped to the bathroom door, grateful for the noise of cascading water, which would allow me to place the emergency call.

But as I reached for the doorknob, his phone vibrated. Loudly. Notifying him of my deception.

He grabbed me, and the phone slipped from my sleeve and clattered to the floor.

He gaped at it, then at me. He seized the phone,

shoved it deep in his pocket, and swore. "You were going to call the cops, after everything I've done for you?" His neck muscles tensed, tendons bulging. He stared at me, and I saw something breaking behind his eyes, like a fantasy shattering.

With a slight shake of his head, he stepped back. "I've always been on your side. You're supposed to be on mine. Instead, you're lying to me." His voice rasped. "You don't think I'm brave, you think I'm a terrible person for trying to help you."

"If you'd just gone about it differently, reported him—"

"Which is what you want to do to me. You think I'm no better than him."

"You killed someone, Dane. I can't just—"

"If you can't understand why I had to, then where does that leave us?" A desperate, haunted look filled his eyes. "What do you expect me to do now?"

"The right thing."

He blinked, like he didn't have a clue what that was.

So I spelled it out. "Let us go." I touched his arm lightly. "What you do after that—turn yourself in or run—that's up to you."

He scoffed and thrust my hand away. "You un-grateful—" He bit off a hateful word. Straightened. Gave me a look more severe than I'd ever seen from him. "I'm in this situation because of *you*." His voice lowered. Nostrils flared. "And you don't even care about me."

"That's not—"

"Not like you care about Perigard." He lifted his chin, gaze steely. "I saved you. You owe me your life. I sure as hell didn't risk everything just so you could end up with some other guy."

"I'm not—"

"Stop lying to me." His eyes practically shot sparks. "I saw you with him. I thought if I could just get you away—" He shook his head, clenched his jaw. "But this isn't going to work. I can't trust you."

My heart thumped. "What are you going to do?"

"You're not leaving me any choice."

The ominous implication chilled my blood. "What about Ella? She doesn't know the truth about you. She loves you."

"She loves everyone."

"Whatever happens to me . . ." I swallowed. "Just promise . . . promise she'll be okay. That you won't hurt her."

The shower turned off, and I heard Ella singing a Disney song.

"Promise," I whispered fiercely, tears pressing at my eyes.

He spoke quietly through gritted teeth. "I don't owe you anything."

"Mommy, can you help me dry off?"

Not waiting for his permission, I slipped into the room and locked it. Much good it would do. The poorly designed lock could easily be turned from the outside, as he'd proven earlier by sneaking in when I was on the phone.

I tried to keep the trembling from my limbs as I toweled Ella down. Steam enveloped me in moist warmth. The room's one window was so tiny, even Ella couldn't escape through it—not that I'd send her out into the frigid wilderness alone.

I wrapped her in the towel and pulled her close.

"Mommy, too tight." She wiggled away.

I kissed her cheek, her clean, warm skin smelling of simple soap. Would the moisture in the air mask the wetness in my eyes? "I love you so much, Ella." *Remember that. Always remember that.*

Even worse than the thought of losing my life was the thought of leaving Ella alone.

But no, she wasn't alone. She was already in God's care.

And so was I.

Remember that. Always remember that.

I lingered as long as I could in that tiny bathroom, brushing her hair much longer than necessary, until she ducked away. "You're going to brush all my hair off!" She opened the door, making my heart leap to my throat.

She trotted to her backpack and pulled out her art supplies. "Will you paint with me?"

Dane stepped to her side. "I bet she will—right after she helps me with something. Okay, kiddo?" He handed me a piece of paper covered with handwriting.

Confused, I scanned it.

"Copy it," he whispered in my ear. He pressed blank paper and a pen into my hands.

"And if I don't?"

He flicked his chin at Ella cheerily laying out her coloring book, paint, and brushes.

Message received.

Nodding, I sat down beside Ella and began writing the words that would set Dane free.

Thirty-One

Dear Dane,

First, thanks for helping us when Ella and I needed a place to stay. You've always been nothing but kind, which is why this letter is so hard to write.

Now that the police have Max, it's only a matter of time before the truth comes out. I know he'll turn on me for a lesser sentence. So I have to escape while I still can. It breaks my heart, but I can't take Ella with me. Make sure Connor's parents get her. Despite our differences, I know they love her and will take good care of her.

I blame Max for all of this. He set his sights on me years ago. I never had a chance, even after I married Connor. Over the years, through secret visits, Max convinced me I was in love with him. He seduced me with promises of wealth. And, I'm ashamed to admit, I was taken in.

Together we planned to get rid of Connor. The night I left with Ella, Max broke in and killed him. Soon after, we met up at his place in Vanishing Lakes and laid low.

But things didn't go the way I imagined. I soon realized I'd made a terrible mistake. Max has a dark side. I wanted to leave him, but he wouldn't let me. I fled to the neighbor's place for help—and Max killed the poor old man because I'd told him too much.

I'm so ashamed and feel so guilty for my part in all this, but I'm too afraid to go to prison, so I'm fleeing. Please don't try to find me.

Tell Ella I'm sorry and that I love her.

Brook

Tears mingled with anger as I wrote the ludicrous confession, the wild lies, the insane deception. Was this how my darling Ella would come to remember me? As a cruel, conniving fugitive who'd plotted her father's murder?

If only I could write the truth.

Dane stepped into my peripheral vision. "Makes perfect sense, doesn't it?"

I set the pen down. "You don't have to gloat." My fingers curled, refusing to resume writing.

He set his hand on my shoulder and spoke in my ear, his breath warm, his tone grim. "I'm not. This isn't what I wanted." He squeezed my shoulder.

I shivered and turned to see the fire had dwindled to glowing embers.

"Mommy, I'm hungry and thirsty."

Grateful for a break, I stood and crossed to the fridge,

then stared at the sparse contents Dane had brought in from his truck.

An idea formed.

I returned to the table with an apple and two cups of milk. Sitting close to Ella, I picked up the thinnest paintbrush. "Shh," I whispered, glancing back at Dane, who was adding wood to the fire. I dipped the brush in milk, shielding the action with my body. "It's a secret message. You can tell anyone but Dane."

Quickly, on the back of the letter, I wrote, *Written under duress. Dane Price is the killer.*

Then, heart pounding wildly, afraid Dane would step back at any time, I blew gently and quietly on the message.

By the time he left the fireplace, the paper was dry enough. I turned the page over and resumed penning the required words.

When I reached the last line, Dane crumpled his copy of the letter and chucked it into the fire. He took my copy and set it in plain view on the countertop. As if ready to be "discovered" by him.

Would Ella ever get the chance to tell someone about the secret message? Would she even remember? It was something to hope for, at least—a remnant of possible justice even if I was no longer alive. Because I had no doubt now that Dane planned to dispose of me. It was only a question of when and how.

I stayed by Ella's side through the rest of the day,

soaking up each moment with her, hiding my tension, giving her so many hugs that she started to protest. And I tried not to imagine what was coming next. My eyes still searched for keys, with no success.

Dane gave us a simple dinner of canned chili. He kept sad, watchful eyes on me—until he stepped into the bathroom.

Then I scrambled, silently searching drawers, still finding no keys or phone. I couldn't even find knives.

Made sense.

Dane knew all too well what damage could be done with a blade.

But knives weren't the only things that were sharp.

I pulled the garbage open and touched the jagged edges of the tin can tops. Those could do some damage. I rinsed one and folded it carefully into a half circle, producing a safe side to hold.

The bathroom door opened. I palmed the metal, eased it into my sleeve, and slid the garbage back in place.

Dane crossed to my side and stood too close. "Isn't it Ella's bedtime?"

Instead of replying, I took her hand and led her into the bedroom while slipping the metal into my pocket. After settling with her on the mattress, I read her a story and couldn't resist adding, "What if the prince didn't come to the rescue? What should the princess do?"

Ella frowned, thoughtful. "First, she should pray. Then she should run. And if she needs to, she should fight—even scratching and pulling hair if she has to." She glanced at me as if I might scold her for adding that part. "She'd have to be brave."

"Yes." I patted her hand. "Yes, she would."

I prayed with her, silently pleading that this wouldn't be for the last time.

Dane lurked in the doorway. His presence didn't bother Ella in the least.

God, let her ignorance keep her safe.

I held her in my lap. "Do you know how much I love you?"

"A lot." The confidence with which she said it warmed my heart.

"That's right. More than anything. More than the snowflakes on the ground and the stars in the sky. More than grains of sand on all the beaches." I rubbed her nose with mine, and she giggled. "Remember that, okay?" I struggled to keep my voice from trembling and my eyes from filling.

All too soon, she fell asleep in my arms. I savored the moment. I remembered all our best times from when she'd first been placed in my arms till now.

She was the best part of my life, my greatest blessing.

Dane stepped in and motioned for me to come with him.

Swallowing, I nestled Ella's head onto the pillow and slid my arms out from under her.

I gave her a kiss, then one more.

Please, God, protect her.

My gaze still lingering, I finally stepped from the room.

Dane closed the door behind me.

"What now?" I asked, trying not to show fear.

"Put on your boots."

He put his on as well, then pulled on his coat, hat, and gloves and opened the front door. "Come on."

I reached for my coat, but he took it.

"You won't need that." His expression remained somber but resolute as he forced me out the door and into the frigid night.

Thirty-Two

Snow cascaded from the sky.

"Let's go." Dane locked the door and started for the trees, a forest of branches tossing madly in the wind.

Besides shivering, I didn't move. "You're taking me out there to freeze to death?" My breath made misty clouds that vanished like tiny, desolate ghosts. "So you can pretend to find the letter in the morning, call the police, and have them think I just took off and was so stupid I didn't even wear a coat?"

"You'll have it on when they find you." He slung it over his shoulder. "They'll think you got lost."

My hair whipped into my face and eyes. "And if I don't walk?"

He set his mouth in a grim line, then opened a pocketknife, lifted my hand, and touched my wrist. "I could make it look like you decided to do away with your problems in a different way."

I swallowed and pulled back. Crossed my arms tight against my body.

"Your choice." He waited with a pained expression. "I'm not trying to make this any harder than it has to be.

I wish you weren't making me do this at all. It's killing me inside."

"Sure it is." I stalked off. "If that were true, you'd think of another way. One that doesn't end with me dead."

He looked at me like I'd struck him. "There is no other way. You don't think I've gone over this a thousand times? It's down to you or me now. And as much as I care about you, I'm not going to prison for you."

"I—"

"Don't waste your breath. It's too late."

I didn't think I could possibly get any colder, but the wind bit my exposed skin with sharp, icy teeth.

"Walking will keep your blood circulating a little longer," Dane said, as if I was supposed to find comfort in that.

Why would I want to prolong this torture?

But human instinct made me want to preserve my life as long as possible. And while I had breath, I still had hope. Had to.

God, help me. Ella can't lose another parent.

We reached the forest. My teeth chattered uncontrollably. Maybe in here I'd be slightly more sheltered from the wind. Moonlight leaked through the branches and illuminated the snow in fragmented patches marred by wavering shadows.

My mind screamed with fear. I tried to tap it down with prayer, with the knowledge I could pull out my makeshift metal blade when Dane least expected.

Perhaps I should have already. If I wasted time waiting for a perfect moment, I'd have no moments left.

But fear held me back. I didn't want to fight him.

What if I lost?

Being brave doesn't mean not being scared. It means you keep going even though you are.

Max's words.

I wanted more than his words. I wanted him. His solid, strong, reassuring presence.

He would know what to do.

But I'd left him to face the police alone. Helped frame him with the false written confession. Now I wouldn't even get to tell him I was sorry.

I looked back at our tracks. "The police will see you walked out with me."

"The fresh snow and wind will take care of that. Plus I'll tell them I went looking for you. But I was too late. So tragic." He paused and moved closer to my side. "I mean it. It is tragic. This isn't what I wanted."

His words stung almost as much as the icy air on my cheeks. What he wanted was for an innocent man to take the fall for his crimes.

I lifted my hands and breathed warmth onto my fingers, then stuffed them under my armpits. I tried to imagine all the snowflakes as little white angel wings. A heavenly army of protection.

Angel of God, my guardian dear . . . ever this night, be

at my side . . . and Ella's.

I prayed she stayed in blissfully ignorant sleep. I couldn't bear to imagine her waking up alone to a strange, dark place. But rather alone than with this man. "Will you really give Ella back to her grandparents?"

"Yes, you don't need to worry about that."

"Did they really hire someone to follow me?" I suddenly hoped it was true, and glanced back as if I might spot a PI tailing us, ready to rush to the rescue.

Dane's mouth moved strangely. "Not officially."

Though my muscles and mind were beginning to feel sluggish, a realization pierced me. "It was you all along."

He didn't deny it, and I knew it was true. How convenient. Everyone had trusted him.

Everyone had been deceived.

"I did it because I didn't want them finding you. I bought you time." He squeezed my arm. "I'm not a bad person." His voice went husky. "If you'd only seen this all from my perspective, we could've been back at the cottage, sitting in front of the warm fire. Making plans together."

I shuddered, a mixture of a shiver and disgust, and yanked my arm away. "Only a bad person would do this. And all those other things. Stalking me, scaring me, framing Max."

I put a hand to my head. My thoughts were scattering, blowing here and there like the snow. My face was going numb, and I feared the cold was steadily reaching deeper, plucking at my senses, my consciousness. Only a matter of time till it stole me completely. If I kept my mind active, would it slow my brain from shutting down? "That day we talked in the parking lot, how did you get to the house so fast?"

"The house? You mean the Mortons'?"

"No, my place. Connor's. I stopped to get something, and someone was there. They startled me, then ran. I thought it was Connor, but it was you."

"That wasn't me. If you saw anyone there, it would've been Shelly." He made a derisive noise. "Wouldn't be the first time she snuck in there to wrap herself in his shirt and cry about him. That woman's got problems." He tapped his temple.

I held in a snarky retort. Who was he to mock anyone's sanity?

"I was never the one trying to scare you," he said. "The emails, the school note, the writing on the window—that was all Ian."

"What about that poor old man? Did you really kill Max's neighbor just so you could plant a body on his property?"

"Of course not. I wouldn't do that." His stride slowed. "Haven't you heard anything I've said?" As if he couldn't stand not justifying himself, he added, "If you hadn't left town without telling me, I wouldn't have had to track you down. I tried to protect you, but you only wanted Perigard.

"You're the one to blame for getting him involved. When I found you at his lake house, the neighboring cottage was the perfect place to watch from. It was empty, till one night the old man showed up. Surprised me. Tried to fight me—can you believe that? He was so frail—I didn't mean to kill him."

His words ran together. I'd never felt such bone-chilling cold.

"Hiding his body on Perigard's property—that just worked out. If you hadn't come across it, I would've called it in anyway. What I really wanted was for them to search and find Connor's wallet. If Perigard was implicated in Connor's death, that would've solved all my problems—gotten him out of the way, satisfied the cops, and you would've turned to me."

I could barely hear him anymore. My feet couldn't take any more steps. Wind howled around me, an extension of the cry I wanted to send out into the cruel winter night, but I was shaking too hard. Drawing air into my lungs was like inhaling broken glass.

Suddenly something surrounded me, sheltering me from the lash of the wind. Arms, Dane's arms.

"I really am sorry, Brook."

I hated myself for craving the warmth that came from this treacherous man. How long did I have till the cold took me?

My freezing fingers fumbled into my pocket, closed on the makeshift blade. Lifted it stealthily.

"I'm sorry too." I slashed at his neck, aiming for the vital artery.

He flinched back with a cry. "What the—?"

He grabbed my hand, seized the metal, and yanked it from me.

I glimpsed a shallow, pitiful cut on his neck.

I'd barely nicked him.

My mind labored sluggishly, wouldn't power my muscles correctly.

He chucked the crude weapon into the trees. His fingers dug into my shoulders, and he thrust me from him like a piece of garbage. I stumbled back against a tree, dizzy.

"Your body's shutting down." His voice floated to my ears. "You're dying. You've probably only got a few minutes left. So say hi to Connor for me. You two deserve each other."

I barely heard him. My vision danced, deceiving me. Could it be? A figure approaching through the blinding snow?

"Max?" I mouthed his name weakly, so overcome with sudden hope that I didn't realize I shouldn't have spoken aloud. I could barely distinguish words from thoughts.

"What?" Dane gave an incredulous laugh and stepped toward me. "Perigard? You think he's gonna save you? You're delirious. He's locked in a cell by now."

"Put your hands up," a strong voice said.

Dane spun, jerking me in front of himself like a shield.

Max. There he stood, yards away. Like an avenging angel. Only he held a gun instead of a fiery sword. Aiming the barrel, he said, "Let her go."

"You shoot, you'll hit her." Dane yanked out his knife and touched it to my neck. I tried not to flinch. "Toss me the gun."

Max hesitated. "The cops are on their way."

"Lies." The blade pricked me. "The gun. Now."

A long second passed before Max flung it at Dane's feet.

Knife still on me, Dane shoved me down as he grabbed the weapon.

Max had only made things worse.

I didn't even try to stand back up.

Max strode forward.

"Stop," Dane commanded, brandishing the gun.

Max halted but yanked off his coat and tossed it to me. A perfect throw.

I fumbled into it, relishing the warmth from his body still clinging to it. I even caught a whiff of his scent.

Such comfort. If only for this moment, I was selfishly glad he'd found me, though I couldn't fathom how he had.

"Hang in there, Brook," he said. "You're strong. You'll be okay."

"You're a fool, Perigard." Dane waved the gun and stepped back. "You should've stayed far away from her. She'll only get you killed. I sacrificed everything for her—

for nothing. She isn't worth it. Instead of killing Connor, I should've let him give her what she deserved."

"Sounds to me like you're the fool."

"Then how come I'm the one with the gun? And you're both gonna die." He took aim. "All the cops will find is that you tried to escape together, but—volatile as your relationship is—one shot the other. The other succumbed to hypothermia. Tragic justice. You'll both still take the blame. And me, I'll walk free."

"Nice plan," Max said. "Except for one thing." He lunged for Dane.

The gun blasted.

Max fell.

And blood seeped onto the snow.

Thirty-Three

Horror shot adrenaline through my veins. I screamed and clambered to Max's side. He lay so still.

Deathly still.

"Max! Max, no." Desperation and loss squeezed my heart. *God, please.*

Dane snorted. "Bravo, you really caught that bullet. Kind of an embarrassing way for a magician to go, hey?" Dane eyed me, then toed Max roughly with his boot. "Idiot."

I struck out at Dane, battering his legs. He stepped away and ejected the remaining bullets into the snow, where they sank into the fresh powder.

He clamped my hands onto the gun. "And now your prints are on it. By the time they find you, you'll be dead too. Poor Ella. She's gonna be devastated."

My head spun, my mind shrieked. I had to stop him. I dug in the snow, searching for the bullets. Found nothing. I tried to open the gun chamber. Failed.

Dane leaned over Max—pressed a hand to his neck. Cursed. "Not gone yet."

"Not even close." Max's fist flew up, smashed Dane in

the face and sent him reeling back. With astonishing speed, he landed several more powerful blows while Dane shouted and struggled. But Max pinned him, making retaliation impossible.

He made it look easy, like he'd done this before and knew all the moves.

He whipped out a bright string of handkerchiefs and bound Dane's hands behind his back till he lay like a colorfully tied gift waiting for the police. I wanted to cheer.

Max collapsed.

I gasped and hurried to his side.

He groaned and lifted a protesting hand. "I'm fine. Just catching my breath." He cracked an eye. "That wasn't my best performance. This bullet's cramping my style."

I bit back a sob. What was the matter with this man, joking at a time like this? "Don't move." Blood stained his side.

He pushed himself up. "You're the one I'm worried about. Did he hurt you?" He pulled me to him, rubbed my arms, yanked off his hat and pulled it onto my head.

"Max, stop moving! You were shot."

"Only with a wax bullet." He shrugged, winced slightly. "A prop."

What? "But you're bleeding."

"I'm sure it looks worse than it is. At that speed and close range, that kind of bullet can hurt, but it's not gonna kill me." He craned to eye it. "At least, I don't think so."

I pulled off the hat and pressed it to his wound before removing the coat he'd given me. "You need to put this back on. The cold—"

"No, you need it."

"I have mine." I grabbed it from the ground where Dane had dropped it at some point. "Now put yours on this instant."

"Yes, Nurse." He eased into it, then lifted a finger. "But you might want to work on your bedside manner. And if I may suggest the optimal way of keeping warm in a situation like this—"

He wrapped me in his arms before I could protest. Not that I wanted to protest. I savored his closeness, his warmth, his smell. Then worried about his wound. "We need to call for help."

"Already did." He pressed his cheek against mine, then his nose. Even the warmth of his breath caressed me. "They should be here any minute."

I tried not to be distracted as he sandwiched my hands in his, making my fingers tingle. "I don't understand. How did you find me?"

He smiled. "Frosty."

I blinked. "Frosty?"

"The rabbit. The new collar. I tried to tell you, I put a tracking chip in it. Did it early this morning after his latest escape. After finding that wallet . . . I had a lot of thinking to do. I think best when I'm working with my hands. Then after the police came—"

"I'm sorry about that." I ducked my head. "I should have stayed with you. I shouldn't have listened to Dane."

I glanced over, assuring myself he was still bound, and saw him struggling and cursing.

"It's okay," Max said, "you were right to get Ella out of there."

"Did they arrest you?" My heart seized and I met his eyes. "You didn't escape from the police, did you?" Was I about to lose him again? Because no matter how justified, they wouldn't overlook that.

"Gotta be honest, that would've been awesome. But no, I didn't need to. Sure, they hauled me in for some intense questioning. Took hours. Did their best to get me to confess. But they didn't have enough to hold me without a confession."

He rubbed my hands, reviving the circulation. "When they finally let me go, I stopped at my place long enough to pull up the tracker and grab the only gun I had left. The only one the cops didn't find when they searched my place. I had it stashed with some magic props in a secret underground storage."

"But how did you know Dane was the one—"

"I didn't. I only suspected. Either way, I needed to make sure you were okay. But when I found Ella alone—"

"Over there!" Flashlight beams cut through the trees, and officers rushed our way.

"Help!" Dane croaked. "I was attacked. I'm injured."

Fear stiffened my spine. He was getting ready to spread his poisonous lies. "What if they still arrest us? Dane's word against ours—"

"Dane's word against himself." Max grinned and tapped his chest. "See, I've got this really cool magic device. You just turn it on and it records everything." He slid it up from his front pocket—a cell phone.

I laughed, then cried, hugging him in grateful relief. He hugged me back with a strength I couldn't get enough of.

The police swarmed closer. "Hands where we can see them!"

I didn't want to let go, still had so much to say. But God willing, there would be time for that. Plenty of time.

Releasing Max, I yelled, "Over here! This man was shot. He needs an ambulance."

"Aw, come on." Max tipped his head back and groaned. "Why'd you do that? Now they're gonna take me away from you."

* * *

Max and Dane were whisked off in ambulances, despite Max's insistence he was fine and amid Dane's exaggerated cries of pain.

As for me, I barely registered the questions about whether I was hurt and how long I'd been out in the cold. All my thoughts turned to Ella.

"My daughter, I need to see my daughter." I hurried inside the cottage, and there she was, sitting on the couch flanked by two officers and holding her bunny. That obnoxious, wonderful bunny with the collar that had led Max to us.

Ella almost dropped the animal when she spotted me. She jumped up and raced to my arms. "Mommy!"

I fell to my knees and squeezed her in a hug like I'd never let go.

"Oh, Ella." I eventually edged back to look at her, smoothing my hands over her hair and cheeks. My precious, precious girl. "Are you okay?"

She nodded solemnly. "This time Max woke *me* up by pounding on the door. He wanted to know where you were, but I couldn't find you. He read your letter, and I told him you wrote an invisible ink secret on it."

She pulled in a quick breath and raced on. "And he held it to a light and we watched the words appear. He told me not to worry, that he would find you, and he called the police and told me I would have to be brave and wait for them. That was scary, but God and Frosty helped me not be too scared."

"My brave girl." I hugged her again. "I'm so proud of you."

An officer watching us seemed to work at making her expression neutral. "Ma'am, do you want to be checked over by medical? And then we need to ask you some more questions."

Of course. But if that's what it took to get everything finally cleared up, I would answer gladly. I only hoped I could do so quickly. Because I needed to get to the hospital and find Max.

Thank him.

And finally tell him what he meant to me.

Thirty-Four

The next hours passed in a blur.

The Mortons showed up at the hotel where the police took me and Ella after questioning.

As much as I wished I could keep the truth from Ella, I knew I couldn't. Gently as possible, I explained that her dad and Dane had gotten into a fight and that Dane was the one responsible for his death.

Her eyes grew round, then angry. "Why didn't he tell us? I thought he was our friend." And then she cried.

She needed all the comfort she could get. For her sake, I was glad when her grandparents showed up. They'd driven through the early morning hours to be with us after the police contacted them.

Grief lined their faces, and I couldn't help feeling sorry for them. Dane, whom they'd welcomed into their home as family, had deceived them in the worst way.

But they were grateful to finally know the truth. I prayed it would help them with closure.

After Ella finally fell asleep, they apologized for suspecting me. "I knew, deep down, we shouldn't have," Barb said. "But we had so much anger. We needed to direct it somewhere."

I understood. It would take time to heal our relationship, but I believed it could be done.

And when Ella woke up, I let them take her to breakfast so I could finally check on Max.

I hurried to the hospital, only to discover he'd been released. So I drove straight to his place.

After knocking lightly, I wondered if I might have to pound on the door. He could very well be sleeping. After the night he'd had, he deserved to be.

But the door swung open.

"Brook." Max's eyes lit up with delight. "If you know how many times I tried calling you in the last few hours, you're probably here to break my phone."

I smiled. "That would be a rather ungrateful thing to do considering you just saved my life. And I would've answered every one of your calls if my phone wasn't broken. The truth is—"

His phone buzzed, and he silenced it, stepping back and ushering me in. "Sorry about that. Just my manager calling again. He won't leave me alone."

"The news is calling you a hero. And they're right." I swallowed. "This could be the comeback you needed." Why was that so hard for me to say?

He frowned and put his hands on my arms. "Making a comeback, living life in the spotlight—that's not what matters to me anymore—"

"Max!" Charlene burst through the front door lugging

a suitcase. "Why are you always freaking me out?" She rolled the bag over and hugged him. "Are you really okay? Tell me everything that happened."

So he did, and I helped, and at the end, Charlene looked grim. "This is all my fault. If I'd never sent Brook here—"

"Don't do that, Char," Max said. "None of it was your fault. And I'm glad I was there when she needed me."

"If he hadn't been," I said quietly, "I wouldn't be here now."

Charlene turned to me, stricken. "Oh, Brook. I didn't mean it like that. I just— Max is always getting into trouble." She looked like she wanted to smack him. "He's had more than enough brushes with danger and death to last two lifetimes." She sighed. "All I want is for him to settle down and live a nice, quiet, peaceful life. I'm telling you, it's the best."

Max tapped her luggage. "What's with the suitcase?"

"I'm staying here for a couple of days to make sure you rest."

He rolled his eyes. "In that case, go ahead and take that bedroom." He pointed to the master. "And start unpacking. It'll take time to organize your clothes by color just the way you like."

"Ha-ha." But she didn't deny it, and I laughed. I'd lived with her, and I knew it wasn't far from the truth.

She grasped the handle of her suitcase, then turned back, serious again. "Is there anything you need first? I could make you a snack or some lunch."

"No, I'm good." Max rubbed his head and sounded distracted. "I really just need a second to talk to Brook."

"Oh." Charlene looked at me, said "Oh" again, and smiled like she'd just discovered some great secret. She held up a finger. "I'm not going far, so call if you need me." She slipped out of sight, her voice fading. "I still can't believe they released you from the hospital. You should be in bed resting."

Max groaned, muttered "Two days of this," and crossed the dining room to the sliding door. He looked at me. "Why don't we go out there?"

"Outside?" I followed him. "Onto the snowy deck?"

"Sure, why not? We're good at withstanding freezing temperatures. And if not"—his lips quirked and he put his arm around me—"I'll keep you warm."

I felt myself blush as we slipped out the door.

Blue sky stretched above the frozen lake, and sun glittered on frosted trees. But all I could focus on was how close I was to Max's side. How right it felt.

I pulled in a deep breath of the crisp winter air, enjoying how it swelled my lungs and soul with a vibrant hopefulness. "I kind of agree you should still be in the hospital."

"Please. It's a minor wound. I'm fine. And I'll have you know I left the hospital at the perfect time. I got to see the cops leading Dane out in handcuffs. Best sight ever. You should've seen the death glare he shot me."

"I'm glad I didn't." I paused, then tilted my head to face him. "I owe you everything, Max. I hope you know how grateful I am."

He touched my cheek. "You don't owe me anything. I'm just glad you're okay. And I'm sorry for everything that guy put you through."

"I'm the one who's sorry. You came here needing a break, a vacation, and look what you got."

"What do you mean? This was such a great vacation, I'm seriously considering making it permanent. Minus the guy who tried to kill us, of course." He winked, then looked back at the house. "Though I've gotta say, I never realized how big this place is until you and Ella left. And how empty. Till the police swarmed in—then I got a little preoccupied. But now—" He cleared his throat. "I guess what I'm trying to say is, I don't want to go back to that. To a life without you in it."

He took my hands. "Maybe this is terrible timing, and it probably is. You've been through so much. I'm sure the last thing you want is to take another risk, but I have to ask. Will you give me another chance? I promise I'll wait for you, however long you need.

"But if that's not what you want, just tell me." He released my arms. "I'll go back to California. I'll distract myself and tell myself I'm fine." His eyes met mine with an honesty that pricked my heart. "But I'd rather be better than fine. I'd rather be here with you and Ella. Because I love you."

Wonder and joy pulsed through me. "Oh, Max, I barely had a chance with you all those years ago. I never thought I'd have a second chance. And now . . . you're telling me I do. We do. And I . . ." I sniffed, attempting a smile that came out more as a chin quiver.

"Hey." He thumbed my tears away. "I wasn't trying to make you cry."

I gave a small laugh. The tears felt good, releasing pent-up years of pain and regret.

Washing it away.

"Don't worry," I said, "they're good tears. And just so you know, I don't see risk when I look at you. Not the way you mean it." I touched his face, fascinated by all I did see, unable to reduce it to words.

But I tried. "I see someone I can trust with all my heart. Who risked everything for me, yet is still willing to walk away if that's what I need."

He nodded solemnly, eyes dimming, and I hurried to add, "But it's not. Because I love you too. I want you to stay. I want to see you every day, talk with you, and laugh with you. And . . . and . . ."

"And this?" He pulled me to him and planted a powerful kiss on my lips, stunning my senses and warming me down to my toes.

I laughed, ending the kiss too soon. "How'd you know?"

Eyes bright with happiness, he cupped my face. "I wish I could say I read your mind. But the truth is, my heart told me." He glanced over his shoulder like he was afraid Charlene may have crept up and overheard him. "Man, I've gone sappy." He shrugged. "But you're worth it."

And he kissed me again.

Thirty-Five

"I hope she's not as nervous as I am." I waited with Max in the dim school auditorium as Ella walked on stage to perform her magic skit.

He covered my hand and gave a reassuring squeeze. "Don't worry, she's a natural."

Perhaps, but only thanks to the hours he'd put in teaching her and helping her rehearse over the last couple of months.

Connor's parents sat one row over. After all their shame and regret and profuse apologies upon learning what Ian had put me through, they'd been surprised but delighted to receive my invitation. It was a welcome respite for all of us after the past week, in which Dane was sentenced. Ian had tried to attack him in the courtroom, and as a result, received ninety days in jail. A far cry from Dane's life sentence, but the Mortons had been through enough. It was good for them to get their minds off the darkness and see their granddaughter shine.

And shine she did.

My pounding heart gradually subsided as I watched, delighted as Ella performed an impressive cups-and-balls trick. Next she poured water into a vase, then tipped it over—but no water fell out. The audience clapped and whistled. My chest swelled with pride as my little girl beamed, her eyes bright and sparkly. Happy. A wonderful sight.

For her last trick, she produced a bunny from a top hat. Not a real one, thankfully.

Frosty was a spoiled bunny now, and I didn't begrudge him his pampered lifestyle. After his part in leading Max to us, Frosty was welcome to live out his days being cuddled, escaping his cage, and crunching carrots.

"Did you like it?" Ella asked when we joined her in the hall after the show.

I swept her into a hug. "I loved it so much, I think we'll have to start calling you The Amazing Ella."

"You were spectacular. And these are for you." Max produced a beautiful bouquet of flowers out of thin air.

Ella giggled and whispered, "I know how you did that!" as she bounced on her toes.

"Man, busted." Max winked and laughed. "How about this one?" He pulled something from behind Ella's ear—a large round pin with a picture of a magic hat and wand.

Though I'd never seen it before, there was something almost familiar about it. "Isn't that the pin you told me about, the one you got as a kid?" The one that meant so much to him.

"She deserves it, and I know she'll appreciate it. Time

to make some new memories," Max said, pinning it onto her as a wave of sentiment swept through me.

"Hey, Ella." A boy from her class ran up to her. "How'd you do all those cool tricks?"

She glanced at Max. "A good magician never reveals her secrets." She waved her bouquet, losing a few petals, and pointed it at Max. "But if you really like magic, maybe you could go to his school someday. He's starting a magic one."

"Magic school? Cool! I want to go there instead of here. Hey, Cooper, there's gonna be a magic school . . ." His voice faded as he took off running through the crowd.

I laughed and turned to Max. "By the time you open, you may have a ten-year waiting list."

Not that the list he had wasn't already lengthy. Judging from that and his enthusiasm and skills, I didn't doubt that the Vanishing Lakes School of Magic was going to be highly successful. He'd come up with the idea after realizing how much he enjoyed teaching Ella. He'd bought a large building and was in the process of working out the details. Best of all, it would allow him to work right here, in the town we'd both grown to love.

We bid the Mortons goodbye, since they wanted to get on the road and make it home before it got too late.

As we strolled outside into the brisk night air, Max asked Ella, "How about we get some ice cream to celebrate your successful performance?"

"Yay!"

The ice cream shop's featured flavor of the day turned out to be Bunny Tracks, which made us laugh as we devoured our double-scoop cones. And when Max drove us back to my small rental home—one that had no problem allowing pet rabbits—Ella said, "Come inside and see Frosty. I think he misses you."

"Can't argue with that." Max climbed the steps and was soon playing with the rabbit on the floor right alongside Ella. Before I knew it, she was pleading with Max to stay for her bedtime story.

He didn't need any convincing.

With each of us sitting on either side of her, holding the book and taking turns reading, she'd never looked more content. She drifted to sleep with a smile on her face before the story even ended.

I brushed wisps of hair from her forehead. "She's been sleeping so well lately. Hasn't even needed me to sleep in here with her."

It was what I'd always wanted for her, to feel secure, loved, and safe. I pressed a kiss to her forehead and closed the book.

"So that's it?" Max asked as we left the room. "You're just gonna leave the story hanging? No happily ever after?"

A smile touched my lips. He couldn't know my past resentment of that phrase. Or that I'd recently grown to appreciate its appeal. After all, what would life be without dreams of faith, hope, and love?

"It can wait for another day." My gaze swept my cozy kitchen and settled on him. The man whose zest for life was contagious. The man who made me feel safe and cherished. The man I wanted to spend the rest of my life with.

He nodded at my table, laden with open textbooks. I'd been devouring them as I began working toward my nursing degree. I'd started some online classes and couldn't wait to take a full load in the fall.

"So what's your happily ever after look like, Brook?"

"This," I said, taking his hands as I walked him to my door. "I'm living it."

"Your idea of happily ever after is kicking me out?"

I laughed at his put-on pain. "Sorry, but I've got to get up early for work tomorrow." After dropping Ella off at school, I'd be handling the bustling breakfast shift at FlapJack's Diner.

"No, you're right. You've gotta kick me out or I'd never go. Not when I could be doing this." He wrapped his arms around me and captured my mouth with his. I savored the kiss, knowing it would keep me warm until I saw him again.

"Man," he muttered against my cheek, "I love saying good night. And I hate it."

"I know." I pulled the door open, and we stepped out onto the stoop. I shivered, but the air was mild for an April night. It smelled of melted snow on pavement and damp earth. The night sky twinkled.

Max took a step away, hesitated, and turned back to me. "What's that?" He brought his hand up to my hair. "I've heard of earrings, but come on, Brook. That's a mighty big rock to be hiding there. It would look a heck of a lot better on your finger."

I gasped at the diamond ring in his hand.

"I thought I could wait to ask you this, but . . ." He dropped to one knee. "I know some guys would plan this out, rehearse for weeks, make it a huge event. But that's not me. All I've got to offer is the diamond, myself, and a lifetime of love. I hope that's enough. Will you marry me?"

His earnest eyes held me captive more than the huge diamond. "Oh, Max, of course. It's more than enough. I don't want some guy, I want you. Only you. Forever."

With a silent cheer, he bounced back up and kissed me.

Took my breath away.

"And you think Ella will be okay with this?" He eased back to see my face.

"More than okay. She loves you too."

He nodded. "I don't want to let you or her down." His brow flickered and he cleared his throat, suddenly worrying me.

His eyes met mine with a shadow of vulnerability I'd never seen in them. Like he was about to disclose his deepest, darkest fear. "I want to be a great husband and dad. But you know mine died when I was young. And my grandfather—he was no example, except of what not to do. My only fear is I'll screw this up. I don't—"

I pressed my fingers to his lips. The unflappable, confident Max had a worry after all. And I loved him all the more for admitting it. "No one's perfect. We'll both mess some things up. But I know we'll be okay. More than okay."

Max nodded, relief relaxing his face. He hugged me and kissed me again. "So when do you want to get married?"

Something furry brushed my ankle. I gave a little shriek and we almost stumbled off the steps. I caught a flash of white go bouncing down the stairs.

"Frosty!" I pointed and laughed. The rascal. "He's telling us he wants a part in the wedding. The ring-bearer bunny."

"So he can run away with the rings? Sounds like a terrible idea."

I laughed harder, then covered my mouth, hoping I hadn't woken Ella or our neighbors. "Come on, we'd better catch him."

We tried, but he hopped and darted with all the energy of a child, seeming to think that making us scramble about in the dark was great fun. Max finally caught him behind a bush, and we deposited him back inside, closed the door, and latched it this time.

"Another great escape." Max shook his head. "Ella really should've named him Houdini. I'm telling you, that rabbit will be the next thing to ruin my reputation. *Magician Outsmarted by Escape-Artist Rabbit.* I'll never live it down."

I held back a laugh. "You know we're a package deal. You'll have to live with that mischievous critter too. Since you're the one who sprang him on me, it's actually quite fitting."

He flicked a twig off his jacket. "What was I thinking giving her that thing?"

"You were thinking of Ella." I softened my voice. "Just one of the reasons I fell in love with you." I drew him to me and kissed him.

A playful glimmer lit his eyes. "In that case, I should probably get more rabbits."

I laughed. "You're impossible."

"Didn't Char warn you about that?"

"Maybe, but you're also irresistible."

"Yeah? Should I bill myself as that for my magic school? The Irresistible Max. Something tells me I'd be laughed right out of business."

"Not by me. I love how you make me laugh." I set my palm against his cheek, knowing that with him, there'd be plenty of laughter ahead. Yet as I snuggled into his embrace, I found myself looking forward to the everyday moments the most—waking up beside him, taking long walks, simply sharing life.

That's where the real magic would be.

A Note from the Author

Though it took me many years to decide to write this story, I'm so glad I finally did. I hope you enjoyed it, and if you did, I'd be so happy if you'd take a moment to share your review on Amazon. Your words really make a difference!

No matter how many times I release a new book into the world, putting it out there still feels daunting and scary. So hearing that someone enjoyed one of my stories always makes my day. I'm so grateful to my readers!

Interestingly, as I was preparing to release this book, I came across an old forgotten poem I'd written as a teen that just so happened to be called "Illusion." Since the theme matched so well, I decided to use it as the epigraph for this book.

My teenaged self would have been thrilled to know I ended up putting that poem to good use instead of leaving it to fade into the past, as did my poetry-writing days.

Here's hoping I still have many more novel-writing days ahead.

Acknowledgments

My decision to finally write a third Frozen Footprints book wasn't an easy one, and I'm so grateful to everyone who encouraged and helped me along the way. I send heartfelt thanks to:

My readers, for your enthusiasm and requests for another book. I'm so glad you wanted Brook and Max to have their own happily ever after.

My amazing sisters, Monica and Cassandra, for all your support, time, and effort in helping transform this story into the best it could be. Your editing and problem-solving abilities never fail to impress me—and save me from embarrassment. A million thanks! I truly couldn't do this without you.

My brother, Jerome, my original Max inspiration and a wonder with a deck of cards, coins, linking rings, and more. I sure wish you were here to read this last book in the series. But you're always in my heart, and I know I'll see you again.

My brothers-in-law Chris and Ray, for taking the time to read my work and give feedback. Your perspective and advice are invaluable to me, and I'm so appreciative.

Finally, glory be to God, whose love is boundless and to whom I owe everything.

About the Author

Therese Heckenkamp was born in Australia but grew up in the United States as a homeschooled student.

She lives in Wisconsin and is now an award-winning author of six romance/suspense novels as well as a non-award-winning mother of five energetic kids.

As a busy mom, Therese fits in writing whenever she can manage (and sometimes when she can't, since somehow her home never stays clean for more than a moment). She dreams up new stories mostly at night when the house is, if she's lucky, finally quiet (which is almost better than clean).

Therese hopes you'll visit her online, where you can check out her other novels, sign up for her newsletter, and be among the first to know when she releases her next book.

Find her at thereseheckenkamp.com
Amazon.com/author/thereseheckenkamp
Goodreads.com/thereseh
Facebook.com/therese.heckenkamp
Instagram.com/theckenkamp

Made in the USA
Monee, IL
10 December 2023

48656085R00163